The Birds and N
of the Sout

by

Gordon Waterhouse

Photographs by Bryan Ashby

Line drawings by Mick Loates

ORCHARD PUBLICATIONS
2 Orchard Close, Chudleigh, Newton Abbot, Devon TQ13 0LR
Telephone: (01626) 852714

All rights reserved. No part of this publication may be reproduced, stored in a retrieval system, or transmitted in any form or by any means, without the prior permission of the copyright holder.

ISBN 1 898964 38 6

First published in Great Britain 2000 by Orchard Publications
ISBN 1 898964 38 6

© Gordon Waterhouse – text
© Mick Loates – drawings
© Bryan Ashby – photographs
© Kenneth Hurrell – photographs page 11

All rights reserved. No part of this publication may be reproduced, stored in retrieval system, or transmitted in any form or means, without the prior permission of the copyright holders.

British Library Cataloguing in Publication Data.

A catalogue record for this book is available from the British Library.

Printed by
Hedgerow Print
The Old Creamery, Lapford, Crediton, Devon EX17 6AE

CONTENTS

ACKNOWLEDGEMENTS

My thanks to Bryan Ashby and Mick Loates for their illustrations
and to Tony Soper for his foreword.
I am indebted to Barbara my wife and friends who read the original
manuscript, the remaining errors being the author's.
My thanks also to the many other naturalists who have shared my
explorations of the South Hams.

To
BILL TUCKER
and
BRYAN ASHBY

Map illustrations based upon Ordnance Survey Mapping by permission of
Ordnance Survey on behalf of the controller of Her Majesty's Stationery
Office, © Copyright MC100031013.

The South Hams – from Dartmoor Tor to
Burgh Island lapped by the sea.

THE SOUTH HAMS

FOREWORD

Travel may broaden the mind but the best of all travel is the few miles you explore from your own back door. Or the front door of your holiday hotel or the flap of your tent! And if you start from a door anywhere within the magic kingdom of the South Hams then you are exploring the cream of Devon. From the rugged edge of Dartmoor by way of family farms, wild woodland, fishfull rivers leading to tidal estuaries and the finest coastline in England, you are enjoying a land blessed by a cornucopia of wildlife.

In discovering a wild landscape to best effect you need a knowledgeable companion. In this book you have found the man best qualified to lead you to the wildest corners of the South Hams, Gordon Waterhouse is a master hand at finding secret places and communicating first-hand knowledge. Go with him through these pages and you will get to know and love this precious corner of an island which, in spite of everything is still a haven for wildlife.

Tony Soper

DARTMOOR WITHIN THE SOUTH HAMS

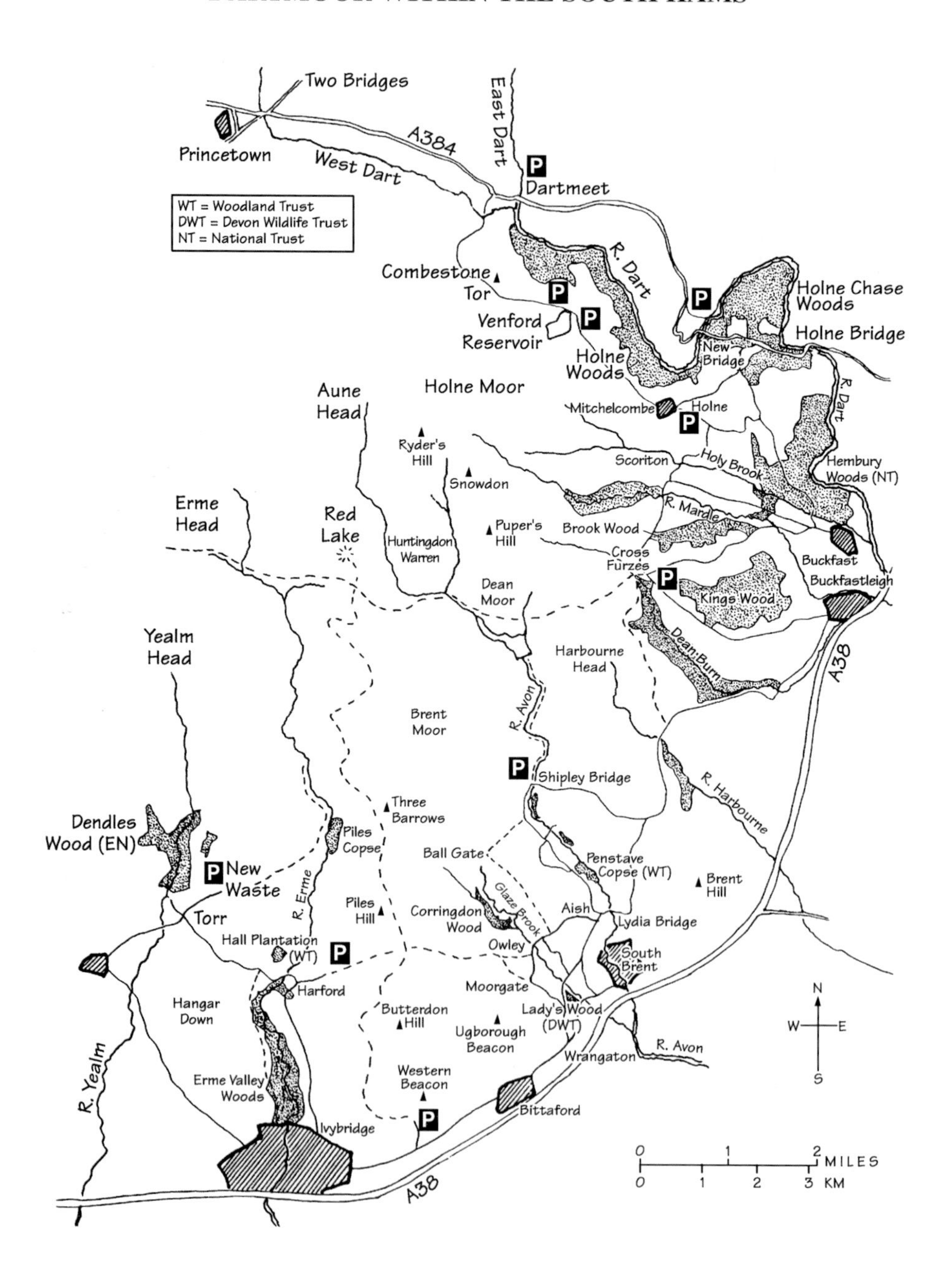

Introduction

We are standing on Brent Hill, on volcanic debris from 300 million years ago. Volcanoes erupted in the shallow seas at the end of the Devonian geological period, spreading lava and ash. From over a thousand feet above sea level, Brent Hill gives splendid views of the South Hams. Before the Romans came, Iron Age peoples built up a rampart, circling the top of the hill to provide a place of safety for themselves and their animals. The grass covered bank and ditch is still there. So are the ruins of St.Michael's chapel, built in mediaeval times for worship and meditation. Today, the buzzard wheels above Brent Hill, mewing in the blustery wind.

From Brent Hill, we and the buzzard can see most of the South Hams. Far to the south, a plateau of hard, metamorphic schist rises, like a blue island, stretching from Start Point to Bolt Tail. Perhaps these are the most ancient of all Devon's rocks. Devon's geology starts here. The upper part of Salcombe shows as a shallow dome, covered in houses. Between us and this distant, ancient plateau is an undulating, patchwork quilt of green and brown fields, the agricultural heart of the South Hams. The quilt is cut into by valleys, steep-sided and often wooded, running from North to South. The rocks of this heartland were laid down in shallow seas, in tropical latitudes about 400 million years ago. Great thicknesses of mud and sand were built up on the sea's floor, over many millions of years. In the deeper parts, limy shells and skeletons of marine animals formed most of the sediment. Pressure, heat and great movements of the earth have converted them to shales, slates, grits and limestones. The softer Meadfoot Slates flank the schist plateau; the waves of the sea have bitten into the soft cliffs and created Start and Bigbury bays. The harder Dartmouth Slates are more resistant, stretching from the high ground above Wembury and Stoke Point, to the west, to the high ground above Froward Point and Kingswear, to the east, where a daymark stands, like Cleopatra's needle. Further east, a ring of houses mark where Torbay meets the sea and the limestone cliffs of Berry Head show as a vertical line; the solidified remains of those limy shelled marine animals from the deeper parts of the Devonian Sea.

To the north of Brent Hill rises Dartmoor, patterned with bracken, dark green in the summer and rusty brown in the winter. Some 290 million years ago Dartmoor slowly rose, a bubble of molten rock, pushing up the layers of Devonian slates and the fringe of volcanic lavas. It did not break through to the surface but solidified as granite. Millions of years of erosion by water, freezing, thawing and flowing, have removed the Devonian rocks and exposed the granite. Around the edge of the giant bubble, is evidence of where the molten rock met the Devonian crust and baked it. In the great Armorican mountain building movement, about 270 million years ago, all the rocks were squashed, folded and refolded, rising above the seas as a range of contorted mountains.

The Permian age followed. In desert conditions, layers of sand and gravel were laid over the Devonian rocks by wind and by flash floods. These formed the rocks we call the New Red Sandstone, the dominant rock around Exeter. Over the South Hams most of it has been eroded away but outliers survive at Slapton and Thurlestone, staining the surrounding rocks red.

Ever since, as our part of the earth's crust has migrated from tropical latitudes to its present position, the climate has ceaselessly changed and sea and rain, fire and frost have sculpted the landscape.

This is the geological setting, which provides the backdrop for the story of the wildlife of the South Hams. The boundaries chosen, are the River Dart to the east, the River Yealm to the west and the South Hams District Council boundary to the north.

The purpose of this book is to share, with visitors and residents alike, the joys of discovering the wildlife habitats within this striking landscape. You have a guide from which to start an exploration of the South Hams and make discoveries of your own.

Brent Hill in the middle distance with the South Hams beyond.

I

DARTMOOR

Common Polypody and Maidenhair Spleenwort

The highest peak in the South Hams is Ryder's Hill (1691 feet: 515 metres). Near here rises the River Avon and within a few miles, the Erme, the Yealm and the Plym. A wide spur slopes gently towards Buckfastleigh, over the lower hills of Snowdon and Puper's. It is high moorland, covered with purple moor grass, deer grass and sheep's fescue. In autumn, when the tussocky purple moor grass has turned the colour of pale straw, I have seen the day-hunting, short-eared owl beating across this moor, looking for voles. His mottled buff and cream plumage matches the subtle colouring of the grasses and his slow, buoyant flight the rise and fall of the Dartmoor winds. Here also is the occasional covey of red grouse, perhaps half a dozen, whirring away on dark brown, arched wings. Flocks of several hundred golden plover gather on the lower, grassy spurs. These are relics of old erosion surfaces. The erosion surface at about a thousand feet above sea level, around Harford, Cornwood and South Brent, is a favourite resting place for golden plover, during the autumn and spring migration.

The wooded coombes are rewarding hunting grounds during migration time. Walks up the Yealm above Tor, near Cornwood, the Erme above Harford and the Avon above Shipley Bridge are often rewarding. There are also good walks up the smaller streams such as the Glaze Brook above Owley, the Harbourne above Gidley Bridge, the tributary streams of the Dean Burn west of Cross Furzes near Buckfastleigh, and the Mardle and the Holy Brook above Scorriton. Here, in the autumn, flocks of redwing and fieldfare arrive from Norway and

The River Avon, near its source.

Sweden, to strip the rowans and holly of their berries. A flock of small, dark-backed thrushes, with a weak call – 'seeep' – as they fly, will be redwing. As they perch in the tree tops, the cream eyestripe shows clearly and the rusty colour of the underwing as they take flight. The fieldfares are larger thrushes, distinguished elderly statesmen, with grey heads. Their rumps are also grey, as they fly, with a chuckling call, their 'armpits' show white. There are extra blackbirds and song thrushes too. A few ring ousels, which have nested in isolated quarries and rocky ravines on high Dartmoor, or in Wales, northern England or Scotland, pause on their southward migration to Spain or the Atlas Mountains; the tart rowan berries provide fuel for the journey. Nowhere are mistle thrushes so frequent as in these Dartmoor coombes, sometimes mixing with their Scandinavian cousins, sometimes in flocks of their own kind. Individual birds or a group will take over a holly tree and guard its berries against all comers, other birds or even humans looking for a sprig for their Christmas pudding. The old Devon name of holm screech, refers to the mistle thrush's love of holly berries and to their harsh call, as off they fly.

Winter passes. There are blizzards of swivelling snow, streams edged with icicles and brittle ice daggers. Seeping water transforms valley bogs into treacherous ice fields. False springs arrive and finger and toe-tingling mornings, with clear skies and every grass blade and twig rimed and glittering with frost diamonds.

Some thrushes and parties of tits and goldcrests still haunt the coombes and lower pasture fields. Robin, wren and dunnock, ubiquitous birds of the hedgerow, appear in unexpected places, where there is a scrap of cover. But up on the moor, it is almost deserted. The buzzard sails on uplifted wings, looking for the movement of rabbits or smaller mammals. Crows and ravens sit on the granite walls and tors, waiting for the deaths that must surely come. Then they

Author crossing a Dartmoor river.

feed on the carrion. Occasionally a whickering cry betrays a peregrine, sweeping across the moor and wheeling high to view a flock of starling or redwing, or an unwary wood pigeon flying over the coombe. Once in a lifetime one may see the vertical stoop and the explosion of feathers as the falcon strikes his prey in mid-air.

So spring arrives. In February the ravens will be bringing beakfuls of sheep's wool to line their nests, in an isolated, moorland tree or on the ledge of a granite crag. Soon after, dippers make their nests under the arched bridges, where country lanes cross the moorland streams. They perch on the moss-blackened boulders, white bib towards you, and flex their knees to make their characteristic, dipping curtsy. Their extra, white eyelid flicks across the eye, as if winking at you. Then they disappear into the water, walking over the bottom searching for stonefly and caddis larvae, seemingly impervious to the force of the current or the laws of buoyancy. When they fly upstream, they keep low, only inches above the water, fast and straight, dark brown back blending with the troughs of shadow in the rippling stream.

The grey wagtail has a bouncing flight, long tail streaming behind; it too is a water bird. As it lands on the rounded, granite boulders, the long tail jerks, vibrates and wags. It feeds by pecking for the insects that are in the black moss growing on the water-worn boulders or in the vegetation at the edge of the stream. Sometimes it hawks over the water, grey wings fluttering to keep it hovering while it snaps up the insects that have hatched from their underwater larvae. The yellow underparts and slate-grey back are bright in spring sunshine.

Up on the moor, where heather, bracken and grasses are still winter shades of grey, brown and yellow, the skylarks and meadow pipits have returned. Only on the moorland is it possible to walk on a spring day and never be out of hearing of the skylark's high-trilling, uplifting song falling from the heavens. The meadow pipits may be even more common but sing less continuously. The children call them 'parachute birds'. When disturbed they give a single, repeated alarm call: 'tsip, tsip, tsip'. When displaying, they fly upwards and begin a song of snatches and trills, which lasts about twenty seconds. The song increases in speed and volume and the pitch rises until, at the zenith of the display flight, the meadow pipit spreads its wings and parachutes downwards. The speed and volume of the song decrease and the pitch lowers, ending with slower, fluting notes, as it sinks to the ground.

By early March, the first wheatears are arriving back from Africa. As with most migrants, the males arrive first. Wheatears not only breed right across northern Europe and Asia but also in the New World, from Greenland to Alaska. Virtually all the wheatears in the world winter in Africa, in the dry savanna country south of the Sahara. Before the quest for correctness began, Devonians called the wheatear 'white-arse'. The grey-backed male will perch on a wall or a boulder, and flick its tail, like its relative the stonechat. As it flies from boulder to boulder, it shows a white rump – its white arse. On Dartmoor they nest in holes in the granite walls or in the clitter, the jumbled granite debris that lies on the slopes below many of the tors. They nest at a greater density on Dartmoor than anywhere in Britain.

The granite provides a lodging for many lichens. The commonest is the beige coloured crottle (*Parmelia saxatilis*), one of the leafy species which clothe rocks and tree trunks and branches with attractive patches of crisp, spreading leaves or flakes of lichen. Another, frequent on large boulders and the higher tors is rock tripe (*Lasallia pustulata*), which grows as circular, grey brown discs, about three or four inches across, smothered in blisters. Matchstick lichens are grey, tipped with bright red fruiting bodies, like the tips of red matches (*Cladonia coccifera* and *C. floerkeana*). They may be on the granite or in the peat around it. Two other grey, bushy *Cladonias* are common on the drier peat and heaps of clitter and tin streaming. They resemble the trees on a miniature railway layout and are closely related to reindeer moss. One leans over to one side (*Cladonia arbuscula*) and one sticks out equally in all directions (*Cladonia portentosa*).

Down in the valleys, spring brings the warblers. In the upper, more open parts of the valley woodlands, during March, the chiffchaffs arrive, singing in the streamside pussy willows. The willow warblers follow in April. Lower down in the oak woodlands, in Dendles Wood, Piles Copse, or any of the wooded coombes, the wood warblers arrive. The Dart valley, from Hembury Woods, near Buckfast, through Holne Woods to Dartmeet, is alive with the wood warbler's song in April and May; a high, staccato trill, unwinding like a clockwork toy. This too is the habitat for the pied flycatcher, another summer visitor. They are restricted to woodland on the edge of moors. The females are inconspicuous, grey-brown birds but the black and white males stand out, singing rather unmusically, on a branch under the canopy, half way up an oak tree. They have increased during the last fifty years and breed readily in nest boxes.

Tree pipit.

At the edge of woodland, is a good place to wait for a redstart. Both male and female have the red tail, which quivers as they sit on a twig or wire fence. Only the male has the startling white forehead, black throat and chestnut breast. Related to wheatears, they too winter south of the Sahara. They nest in a hole in a tree or in a stone wall. The whinchat is in the same family and also migrates to sub-Saharan Africa. It has a different niche. In Britain it is near the southern edge of its breeding range, whereas the stonechat, is nearer the northern limit of its range. Whinchats nest in tussocky grass, often close to gorse bushes, on which they perch. They are commonest near the heads of the valleys. The male stonechats, with their black head and white collar, are conspicuous as they perch on the top of the gorse or a bracken frond. More often, they nest low down in gorse bushes.

At the edge of woodland tree pipits sing from the tops of birch or oak and continue their song in an aerial display. They nest on the ground like their cousins the meadow pipits. Unlike the meadow pipits they spend the winter in Africa.

Some of the valley sides are awash with the blue of bluebells and during May the Erme, between Harford and Piles Copse, is a picture. After the bluebells have finished flowering, the green shepherd's crooks of the bracken rapidly overtop them, spread out their fronds and provide shade, just as the oak trees do down in the valley woods.

In the shorter cropped grassland, the yellow, five-petalled flowers of tormentil star the ground. The small flowers of milkwort – pink, blue or white – and later, the trailing stems and white flowers of heath bedstraw give a speckling of colour. In the damper grassland, are the almost stemless, hooded pink flowers and ferny leaves of the lousewort, once valued as a protection from the lice that waited in one's bedding. The heathers are less extensive than they were a generation ago but they and the summer gorse still provide vistas of purple and yellow on some of the higher slopes, in mid and late summer. The cross-leaved heath, which grows in wetter ground, has the largest flowers – pale pink bells. The bell heather has rich, deep purple bells and the ling has smaller flowers in delicate, mauve spikes. Bell heather, ling and the juicy-berried bilberry require better drainage and quite often grow on the prehistoric banks of the Bronze Age enclosures and hut circles. Dartmoor is one of the richest areas in Europe for visible remains of Bronze Age settlements. They also grow on the oval pillow mounds, constructed by the tin workers as warrens for rabbits, to provide a cheap source of fresh food. The remains of 'tin streaming' have created hummocky valley bottoms, with piles of pebbles, partly covered with grey, bushy *Cladonia* lichens and heather.

From early mediaeval times, men diverted the streams to gather the heavier tin pebbles for smelting and piled up the rejected ones. Wheatears often perch on top of them.

Patches of bog develop in the valleys, on the flat hilltops and on slopes where springs seep out of the peaty ground. The bright green of sphagnum moss shows where the terrain is wettest. In May and June, the white heads of the cotton grass wave above the sphagnum. This is snipe territory. In mild weather in the winter they probe their long bills into the soft moss and peat, to feed. In summer a few pairs nest in these boggy areas. The males tower into the sky and dive down, with their outer tail feathers extended, making a bleating sound, to attract a mate and proclaim their territory.

If you have boots and are not too bothered about getting wet feet, the bogs have a beautiful flora to explore. Early in the year the white bog crowfoot, with its creeping stems and ivy-shaped leaves, is in bloom. Later, another buttercup, the lesser spearwort, with thin, spear-shaped leaves, is common. There is a small violet, the bog violet, which has delicate purple veining on its pale flowers. By midsummer, the tall, yellow spikes of bog asphodel are in bloom. Its scientific name of 'ossifragum' (bonebreaker) gives a graphic picture of cattle or ponies, stuck in the soft peat of the bogs, where the ashodel grows, and straining till they break their legs and die a lingering and cold death. Walkers beware!

On bare patches in the bogs, you can find an insectivorous plant, the sundew. Its round leaves are covered in long, reddish hairs, each with a minute drop of sticky dew at the tip. Midges and flies landing on these leaves are trapped by the sticky 'dew'. The plant absorbs the nitrogenous nutrients from the tiny corpses, which supplement the poor supply of available nitrogen in the waterlogged bog. A much less common insectivorous plant, is the pale butterwort. It has a rosette of flat, triangular leaves; these are sticky and curl over at the edges to trap small insects. This plant is one of the Lusitanian flora species that are restricted to the south-western Atlantic coast of Europe. You can look for it in the boggy patch to the left of the road leading up to the Avon Dam, about two hundred yards north of the Shipley Bridge car park – always a good place to start a walk. Creeping along the boggy surface are two typical plants; marsh pennywort, with circular, crimped leaves and bog pimpernel, with delicate pinnate leaves and pink flowers. Ivy-leaved bellflower is another trailing plant, growing at the edge of the boggy patches and in wet grassland. Its blue bells speckle the turf in late summer.

Another south-western plant is the rare filmy fern, which is found in the shade of mossy boulders in the wooded moorland valleys. Walking up the Dart valley from New Bridge, or up the Erme valley to Piles Copse provide good sites for the filmy fern and other woodland ferns and mosses. The mosses of Dartmoor are a delight. On the open moor are the wefts of the red-veined *Pleurozium shrebberi* and the dark green tussocks of *Polytrichum* mosses, like miniature fir trees. Within the woodlands are mats of another red-veined species *Rhytidiadelphus loreus* and pale flattened fronds of *Plagiothecium undulatum*; their very names evoke an atmosphere of magic.

A few hundred yards north of Huntingdon Cross, on the east bank of the Western Wella Brook, is a rectangular depression, the remains of primitive stone-walling and a stone with an incised cross. Some have thought it dates from mediaeval times but it does not. It is a makeshift chapel made by Rev. Keble Martin and his relations when, as young men, they made annual camping visits to the moor. Throughout his adult life he worked as a conscientious priest but his hobby was the study and painting of plants. He edited the Flora of Devon, which was published in 1939. In 1965, when he was 88, his paintings of the British flora were published as *The Concise British Flora in Colour*. The book

Keble Martin's Chapel, with his flora and autobiography.

topped the bestseller list for months and Keble Martin became a national celebrity. The chapel remains as a reminder of a great and humble man. All over Dartmoor there are granite, drystone walls. Some of the old walls, that run down off the moor, are following the Bronze Age land boundaries; the reave system which may be 3,000 years old. Other walls mark, in geometrical patterns, the small fields at the edge of the moor. Some walls converge as funnels, to guide the stock as they are brought down off the moor. All these walls have an attractive cloak of lichens, mosses, spleenwort and polypody ferns and, in May and June, starry clusters of pink, English stonecrop flowers and rusty red spikes of sheep's sorrel.

Small heath butterflies, small and pale orange, flutter along in front of you. Dark green fritillaries fly strongly. Day flying moths are common, especially male fox moths, large and dark brown. The males fly by day and the females by night. "When do they meet?" asked one inquisitive young naturalist. Their caterpillars are a lovely velvety black with narrow orange bands. You may see the emperor moth's big green caterpillar, with black, hairy spots, feeding on heather. In the autumn, the yellow-striped broom moth caterpillar is very common. From dusty pathways, green tiger beetles take off on brief, whirring flights, especially on hot sunny days.

Within the walls, stoats and weasels live. I have seen the black-tipped tail of a stoat disappear into a hole and, a few seconds later its sharp, inquisitive face has reappeared, peeping over the top of the wall. They feed especially on the abundant rabbits and voles.

On the edge of Dartmoor, at Moorgate, lived H.G.Hurrell, until his death in 1981. Moorgate, north of Wrangaton, is another good starting point for a wildlife walk. H.G. was a naturalist, photographer and author of international repute but the South Hams was his home. Moorgate was also home to many creatures, which he kept 'tame but free' – the title of one of his books. His swimming pool was playground, over the years, to Topsy and Turvy, his two otters and to Atlanta, a grey Atlantic seal. His daughter Elaine and two sons, Leonard and Kenneth,

Above: H.G. feeding a fish to Atlanta at Moorgate in the snow.
Below: H.G. and Black Rod in conversation.

Photographs: Kenneth Hurrell

retain their passion for natural history (as do his grandchildren). They nursed and fed the starved and stranded seal pup, with a stomach pump, using a mixture of milk, margarine, fish meal and cod liver oil. It had been rescued from the mud banks at Newton Ferrers. For over ten years it lived at Moorgate, learning to perform elaborate tricks in return for food and giving every appearance of enjoying life. Atlanta was much visited by local groups, from schools to W.I.s and Tony Soper swam with her in the swimming pool, taking film for the B.B.C.

Tony Soper also came to record the sound of a roost of more than 50 ravens, in the wood by H.G.'s home. H.G. had kept several ravens as pets. One of them, Black Rod, used to go for walks with him, flying off and chasing rooks, crows and later even stampeding cattle and ponies. His freedom had, eventually, to be restricted. When he saw a young hiker taking off his boots and socks to cool his feet in a stream, Black Rod flew down and thought it a great game to try to peck, with his dagger bill, at the man's bare feet.

One winter's morning in the 1970s I was walking over Huccaby Bridge. In the rushing water, which was swirling round the granite boulders, were two ducks with long and hooked, red bills. The drake had a green-black head and white breast; the duck was brown headed with a cleanly defined, white chin. They were goosanders. During the 1970s they were seen more and more often, in the wintertime, on the Dartmoor stretches of the Dart. They began to use Venford reservoir as a roosting place at night. Then, in 1980, a pair nested on the upper Dart, below Two Bridges. It was a few years later that I was walking by the Dart, below Bellever Bridge, one evening in June, with a group of children. We were staying for the week at Bellever youth hostel. As we walked along, suddenly, almost in unison, we froze. On the other side of the river was a female goosander with fifteen black and tan ducklings clustered around her on the water. She pushed downstream with her aft-mounted, orange legs and the young paddled furiously, jostling to keep position near their mother. The children and I were enthralled.

Now, every year, a few pairs breed on the Dart. Every winter they are becoming more common on all our South Hams rivers, almost down to the tidal stretches. The goosander only started to breed in Britain in 1871, having arrived from Scandinavia. Since then it has spread steadily southwards from the north of Scotland.

The red-breasted merganser is a very similar, saw-billed duck, although the green-black head of the drake has a jagged crest and a rusty brown band across his breast. Mergansers have always bred in the northern parts of Britain but recently they too have been expanding southwards and in the early 1990s first bred in Devon. They nest by moorland rivers but move to the estuaries in winter.

Goosanders are occasionally seen on the Avon reservoir. This reservoir was built in 1957 but it is still bleak. Little bird life is attracted. At the shallow, upper end, where rushes grow down to the water's edge, small numbers of mallard and teal and probing snipe gather. I have seen a few goldeneye and cormorants but most often it is birdless. One winter day, in a blizzard, I saw a peregrine fly over the reservoir and disappear into a whirlwind of snowflakes.

In contrast, Venford reservoir, built in 1906 to supply Paignton with water, is a delightful freshwater lake. It is surrounded by conifers – mostly Sitka spruce, rowan and sallows. In addition to roosting goosanders, it attracts mallard, teal, goldeneye and cormorants. Once a great northern diver stayed for some time. In the trees goldcrests are common and sometimes siskins. In summer chiffchaffs and willow warblers sing from the grey-green sallows.

On the slopes above both reservoirs there are good pickings of bilberries in the warmth of July. As summer ends the upper fringe of bracken begins to turn rusty brown. The families of swallows leave the shaded, granite barns, where they have raised their broods. Warblers, redstarts and wheatears all start migrating south and one frosty morning in October, a few redwing and fieldfare are back, feasting on the rowan berries.

Redwings and Fieldfares

II

RIVERS AND STREAMS

Dipper

Rivers are long-lived; their courses may change but they continue – "Men may come and men may go, But I go on for ever," says The Brook, in Lord Tennyson's poem.

The main rivers are the Yealm, Erme, Avon and Dart. There are useful valley trails, produced by the environment section of South Hams District Council, on the Erme and Dart and part of the Avon. There are also rivers in miniature, such as the Harbourne and the Gara and countless attractive streams. They have all excavated steep coombes that are such a feature of the South Hams.

The fringing flora of the rivers and streams is varied. The wide green leaves of great woodrush carpet some shady banks from Dartmoor to the sea. It has distinctive white hairs along the edges of the leaves and grows in moorland, as above Shipley Bridge by the Avon, in many woodlands, as in the Erme Valley woods at Ivybridge, or by the sea, below Noss Mayo on the Yealm. Below New Bridge, on the Dart, the beautiful royal fern grows by the riverside, sometimes almost six feet high. It is often grown in water gardens for its decorative golden fronds. Also near New Bridge, on damp banks and overhanging rock faces, are good sites for Cornish moneywort; very much a south-western plant. The round hairy leaves are similar to marsh pennywort. Snowdrops and daffodils are naturalised in many places near the water courses. They may be truly wild in some sites. Along the riverside path between Yealmpton and Kitley, the snowdrops are a picture in January and February – thousands of green-veined, nodding heads, sprinkled like flakes of snow. By the Avon, near Gara Bridge, is a good site for the pale, wild daffodils, described by Wordsworth. In spring, by all the rivers, there are golden patches of marsh marigold and the pale lilac flowers of ladies' smock scattered across the damp grassland. The orange-tip butterflies lay their small, orange, rugby ball eggs beneath the ladies' smock flowers. Ladies' smock, or cuckoo flower, is in the cress family, closely related to hairy and wavy bittercress. Wavy bittercress is a wavy-stemmed, insignificant, white flower, common along the wet stream banks. Watercress grows with its feet in the water of stream and rill, often with little iridescent green leaf beetles feasting on its leaves. There is also plenty of fools' watercress, which is paler, has leaves more like a parsnip, and umbellifer flowers. By mid-summer the lush, celery-like foliage of hemlock water-dropwort, dominates the water's edge flora. It too is an umbellifer, with big umbels of white flowers. Like fools' watercress, it is poisonous. A very small amount of the white root will kill cattle, sheep and humans.

Water mint, marsh ragwort and marsh woundwort are frequent species. One often smells the water mint before seeing it. The yellow monkey flower, *Mimulus*, with red freckles in the throat of the flower, occurs in patches by the water. This is a naturalised plant, originally from America. Another American immigrant is pink purslane, cheering our banks with its pink flowers, near and not so near water. Rare in the 1920s, it is now very common. At the foot of damp banks the tall lilac-white flowers of common valerian and the creamy, honey-scented meadowsweet blossom. By the end of the summer the Himalayan balsam has grown nearly head high, with dangling pink-purple flowers like Greek heroes' helmets. The fruits that follow swell until, at a touch, they explode, sending the seeds shooting out to float down stream or land on the muddy banks. The Victorians introduced it as a garden plant, from its native riversides in northern India. Out on the gravelly islets and spurs, made as the rivers meander down their course, yellow marsh cress grows and flourishes, until the autumn floods rip away the roots. In the rivers themselves, the green

Himalayan Balsam.

hair of river water crowfoot streams in the current and is jewelled with white flowers.

Alder trees, purple twigged and catkinned in the winter, and thickly leaved in the summer, with green, oval cones, line most of our waterways. Sometimes I have seen the alder fly resting on their leaves; a sturdy insect, with wings veined like leaded glass, held tentwise over its body. Down the middle reaches, where the rivers have left Dartmoor behind, the trees can still grow right across the widening rivers. Walk up the Erme from Ivybridge or down the Avon from Lydia Bridge or Avonwick and see the beech trees, stretch wands of delicate green over the horseback-brown, rippling water.

The granite and peat of Dartmoor produce acid and impoverished stream water. There is no rich supply of calcium, sufficient to build the shells of crayfish and for the same reason the number of species of snail are restricted. However our waterways are, in general, unpolluted. The upper reaches have a bed of granite boulders and gravel, the middle reaches have flattened ovals of Devon slate. As a narrow flood plain develops and the river begins to meander, increasingly there are beds of silt in the bays and curves, where the flow slackens. Living on the surface film are pond skaters, long legs taking them across the water in rapid jerks, as they feed on the floating, dead bodies of emerging insects come to grief. Close examination often shows one skater to be a mating pair. They gather on the slack water in the lea of bridges, fallen trees and by the water's edge. Whirligig beetles gyrate, in silvery circles on the surface film in similar places. Below the surface the water boatmen, row down through the water with legs like oars, and water beetles forage underwater in these calmer habitats. Tiny wriggling midge larvae and the swarms of adults, hanging like clouds over the water and round the trees and tall plants, are abundant everywhere, even in mid-winter. The 'two tailed' stonefly nymphs are commonest in the upper reaches. Different varieties hatch through most of the year. The slender adults have the wings curved down their body, making a silvery black cylinder. The three tailed mayflies are common throughout. Their nymphs are called duns and spinners in the angler's vocabulary. The flattened varieties are commonest in the rapid waters, while the biggest, the fisherman's 'greendrake', needs silt for the big grey nymphs to make their burrows. There are many varieties of caddis larvae. Some have stony cases, made with grains of sand; some are attached to the stones, others are carried about as the larvae forages. Many varieties make their cases of pieces of stick or plant stem, while others have no case at all but construct a web between stones and sit, like a spider, waiting to catch what the current sweeps into it. Damselflies, the blue-tailed and the smoky winged, metallic-green demoiselles, are common along the middle and lower reaches. Patrolling the banks, are the dragonflies, the giants among the riverside insects. It is easy to imagine these, when they evolved to an even greater size in Carboniferous times, winging between lofty horsetail trees, above the coal age swamps. There are the blue green chasers, the wide bodied chaser with golden half moons along the edge of the steel blue or rust brown body or the biggest of all, the black and yellow, golden-ringed dragonfly, *Cordulegaster boltonii.*

Follow the paths by the Erme, between Sequers Bridge and Ermington, by the Avon downstream from Avon Mill nursery, near Loddiswell, or the Dart through the grounds of Dartington Hall and you will see many of these plants and insects.

The cut off meander on the Avon, downstream from Loddiswell, has the atmosphere of a prehistoric swamp and a wonderfully rich flora and insect fauna. Here, as in many other quiet backwaters at the edge of the streams and rivers, you can find the frightening and fascinating water scorpion. He is not a miniature prehistoric monster but a bug with a long tube, protruding like a sting from his velvet black abdomen. This tube has no aggressive purpose; it is merely a snorkel for breathing.

Feeding on the invertebrate life, under water, are the fish. There are both brown and sea-trout varieties of trout. The brown trout stay in the freshwater reaches throughout their lives. Their dappling of vermillion spots makes them particularly attractive; one of Mick Loates' favourite fish. The sea-trout have evolved a migratory pattern, leaving the rather acid river water, with its relatively impoverished fauna, for the rich pickings of the sea. When they are ready to spawn they return to the river and are easily recognised by their larger size and silvery colour. Atlantic salmon, the finest of fish, have a similar migration, returning to spawn in the granite gravels – 'the redds' – high up the rivers, where they themselves were born. In autumn, after heavy rainfall, pause for an hour or so on one of the many bridges over the rivers and you may see that grand sight of a salmon working its way upstream.

From the muddy estuaries to the moorland streams, you may see the sinuous eel, that most amazing fish that drifts across from its birth place in the Sargasso Sea. They spend most of their lives in our rivers, lakes or ponds until they finally make the return migration, to spawn and die in the Sargasso; almost a mirror-reversal of the salmon's life story.

Under the stones of the rivers and streams the bullheads and stone loach rest. Bullheads are often called miller's thumbs, from their size and shape. The middle reaches, where so many watermills used to be sited, are the best for both

Salmon

these fish. The record is preserved in the place names, even though the millers have gone and the mills are virtually all defunct: Knap Mill, Gara Mill, Bow Mills, Mill Leat, Brent Mill, Sheepham Mill, Lee Mill and dozens more.

A friend, who has lived in the South Hams all her life, remembers catching stone loach in the village stream more than fifty years ago and calling them "catabirds". It is a good local name for the fish, which has whiskery barbels around its mouth and broad pectoral fins, like stunted wings.

In calmer backwaters and shallow bays are three-spined sticklebacks and shoals of minnows.

Parasitising all these fish, and so feeding indirectly on the waterweeds and invertebrates, are brook lampreys. They resemble eels but have a circular sucker, instead of a normal mouth, to attach themselves to the flanks of other fish and absorb nutrition through the host's blood supply, until they have outgrown it. Sometimes you may see a fish with a circular scar on its side; this will have been caused by a lamprey.

The whistle of an otter was part of the night-time sound world of the South Hams, until the 1950s, when they became increasingly rare. H.G.Hurrell's two otters, Topsy and Turvy, made spectacular midnight dives from the diving board into his swimming pool. His daughter, Elaine, made a special study of wild otters in the South Hams during that decade and published a book, *Watch the Otter*, about her findings. With the help of the station master at Topsham she recorded electronically how often the otters visited a sprainting stone on the Avon at Topsham Bridge. In the 1990s the otters have begun to make a welcome return. There have been regular sightings on all our rivers. If you look on flat topped stones near the water's edge you may well see the droppings – spraints – of an otter, with fragments of fish bone. If the dropping is dark and curled, it is more likely to be a mink spraint. Mink are usually dark and much smaller than otters. They originally escaped from fur farms and have spread successfully as a wild species in the south-west. They do not seem to have caused the decline of the otter or be hindering the otter's return. Whatever the cause of the otter's decline, the recovery indicates that the rivers are generally healthy.

Wherever top predators thrive, it is an indication of a diverse food-web with a numerous population of smaller species.

At dusk, bats flitter over the rivers, snapping up the insects. The smallest and commonest species is the pipistrelle and the largest is the noctule, which lives in hollow trees. Daubenton's bats are specialists at feeding over water.

Several birds are specialist feeders by stream and river. Each has its own method of fishing and its preferred prey. The few goosanders catch young trout or salmon. Research has shown that they seldom have a significant effect on numbers of fish growing to adulthood. Cormorants have taken to fishing higher up the river and catch larger fish. The heron wades or waits in shallow water, statuesque and bleached as an old fence post, before lunging forward to seize an eel, a frog or any fish that swims within range. The kingfisher, that nests in the sandy banks of the rivers, is just as patient. It watches from an overhanging branch and dives into the water to snatch bullheads, minnows or sticklebacks. The kingfisher is the smelliest but most beautiful bird of the river. Its nest hole stinks of rotten fish but the blue head, back and wings and rich chestnut underparts are a sight to make you draw breath in wonder.

Birds feed on the invertebrates too, in and over the water. Swallows and martins dip low to catch the hoards of midges. A few pairs of sand martins still nest in the silty banks of the lower Avon. The dipper takes his share of the invertebrate harvest under the water. In March and April look under the bridges that span our rivers; many have a dipper's nest, round and untidy, perched on a ledge under one of the arches. Dippers nest early – their food supply is there in the river, whether spring comes early or late. A beakful of caddis, stonefly or mayfly larvae will satisfy the growing brood.

The wagtail of river and stream is the grey wagtail. They also often nest under or near bridges, in a hole or overhang. They cannot perform the dipper's miracle and walk underwater but they search the water's edge and the riverside vegetation for emerging midges, flies and other creepy-crawlies. They can hover in mid-air and snatch a flying insect. We watched a pair by the attractive bridge over the Erme at Harford. While we were having a picnic among the bluebells, the wagtails were walking over the slabs of rock by the river, long tails wagging, slate grey backs and brilliant yellow underparts shining in the sun. With a beakful of insects they flew up, time and again, to the overgrown bank by the bridge,

Avon Mill Bridge.

where their nest of hungry babies was hidden. Suddenly the "chack-chack" call of a magpie alerted us. There was the magpie perched on the parapet of the bridge, with a grey wagtail, in frantic, dancing flight around it. The magpie flew straight to the bank, thrust its head into the undergrowth and flew out with a nestling in its beak. We instinctively stood up and shouted. Both parents mobbed the robber, as it flew across the river. The magpie opened its beak and the nestling fell. It dropped into the river and was swept away in the peat-brown water. Magpies and others in the crow family have their natural place in the pattern of life. Nestlings are as much a natural prey as is carrion from the roadside or ticks from a sheep's back. But we had no love for that magpie.

The pied wagtail is common throughout the South Hams, by farms and villages and by the coast. They often hunt for insects by the rivers and streams, hence their country name of dishwasher. In spring, their black and white patterned plumage, as they dance along the water's edge, makes them look dressed for a dinner-dance rather than for the washing up.

RIVER YEALM

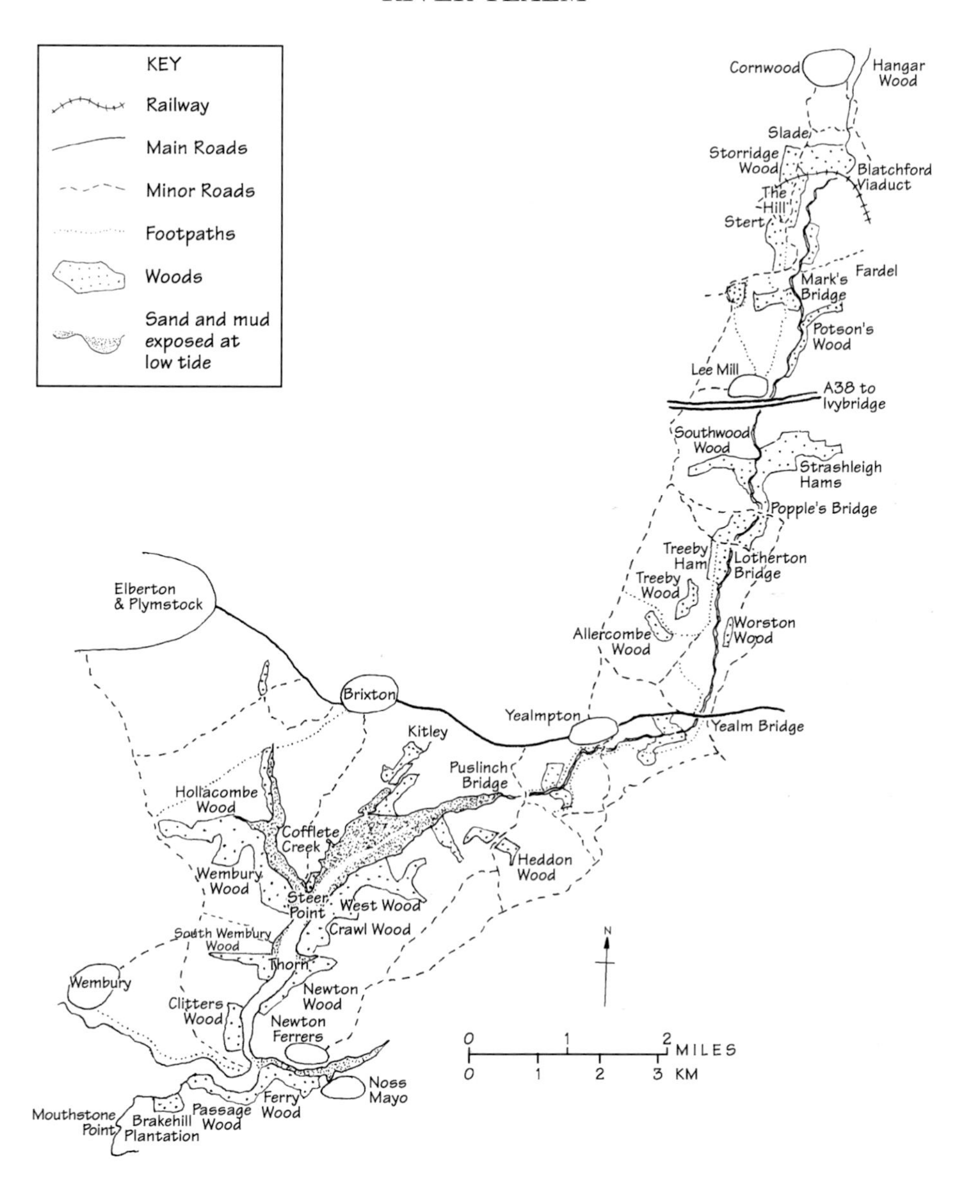
KEY
Railway
Main Roads
Minor Roads
Footpaths
Woods
Sand and mud exposed at low tide
Cornwood
Hangar Wood
Slade
Storridge Wood
Blatchford Viaduct
The Hill
Stert
Fardel
Mark's Bridge
Potson's Wood
Lee Mill
A38 to Ivybridge
Southwood Wood
Strashleigh Hams
Popple's Bridge
Treeby Ham
Lotherton Bridge
Treeby Wood
Worston Wood
Allercombe Wood
Elberton & Plymstock
Brixton
Yealmpton
Yealm Bridge
Kitley
Puslinch Bridge
Hollacombe Wood
Cofflete Creek
Heddon Wood
Wembury Wood
Steer Point
West Wood
Crawl Wood
South Wembury Wood
Thorn
Wembury
Newton Wood
Clitters Wood
Newton Ferrers
Noss Mayo
Ferry Wood
Passage Wood
Brakehill Plantation
Mouthstone Point
N
0 1 2 MILES
0 1 2 3 KM

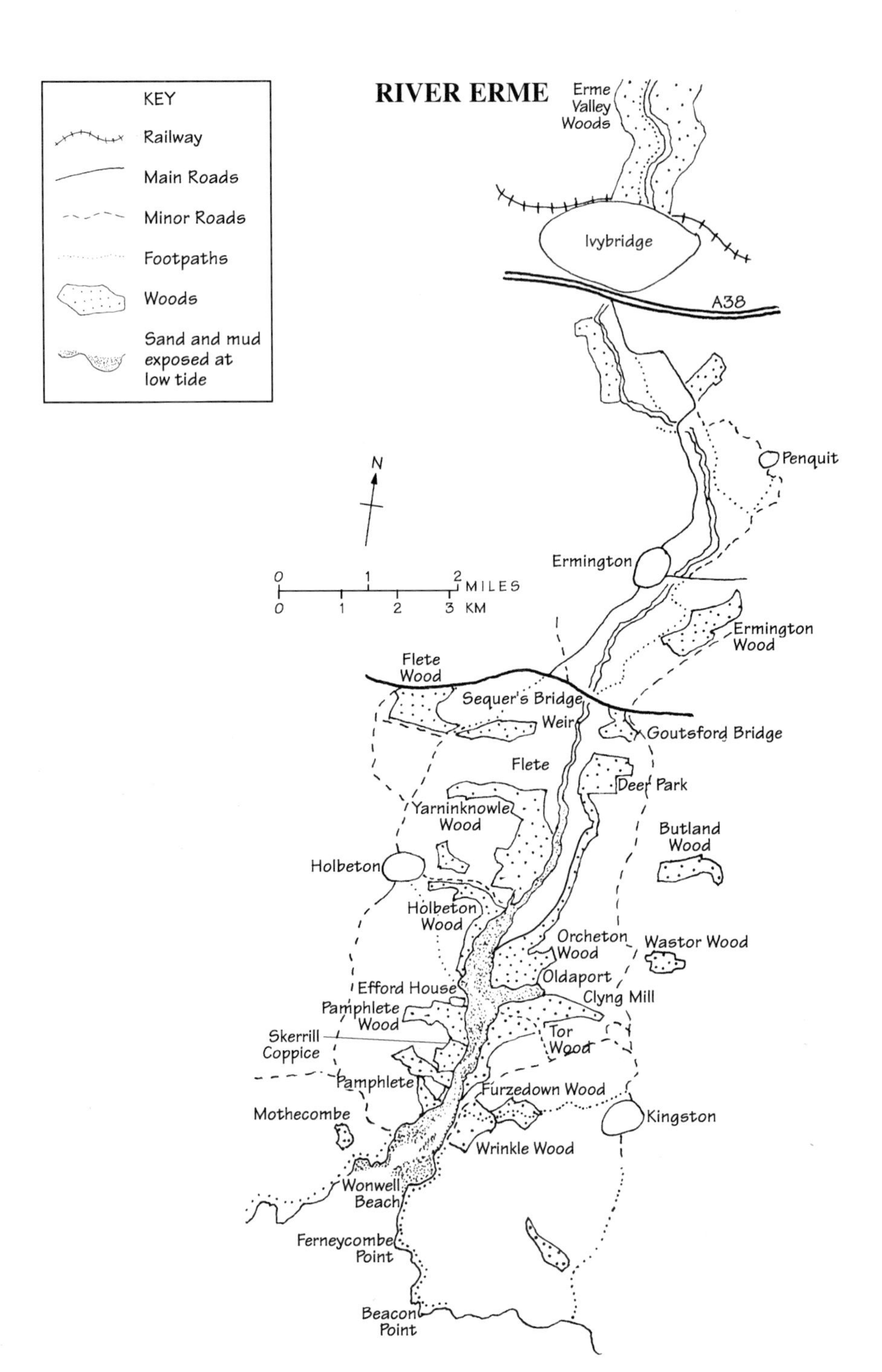
RIVER ERME
KEY
Railway
Main Roads
Minor Roads
Footpaths
Woods
Sand and mud exposed at low tide
Erme Valley Woods
Ivybridge
A38
Penquit
N
0 1 2 MILES
0 1 2 3 KM
Ermington
Ermington Wood
Flete Wood
Sequer's Bridge
Weir
Goutsford Bridge
Flete
Deer Park
Yarninknowle Wood
Butland Wood
Holbeton
Holbeton Wood
Orcheton Wood
Wastor Wood
Oldaport
Efford House
Clyng Mill
Pamphlete Wood
Tor Wood
Skerrill Coppice
Pamphlete
Furzedown Wood
Mothecombe
Kingston
Wrinkle Wood
Wonwell Beach
Ferneycombe Point
Beacon Point

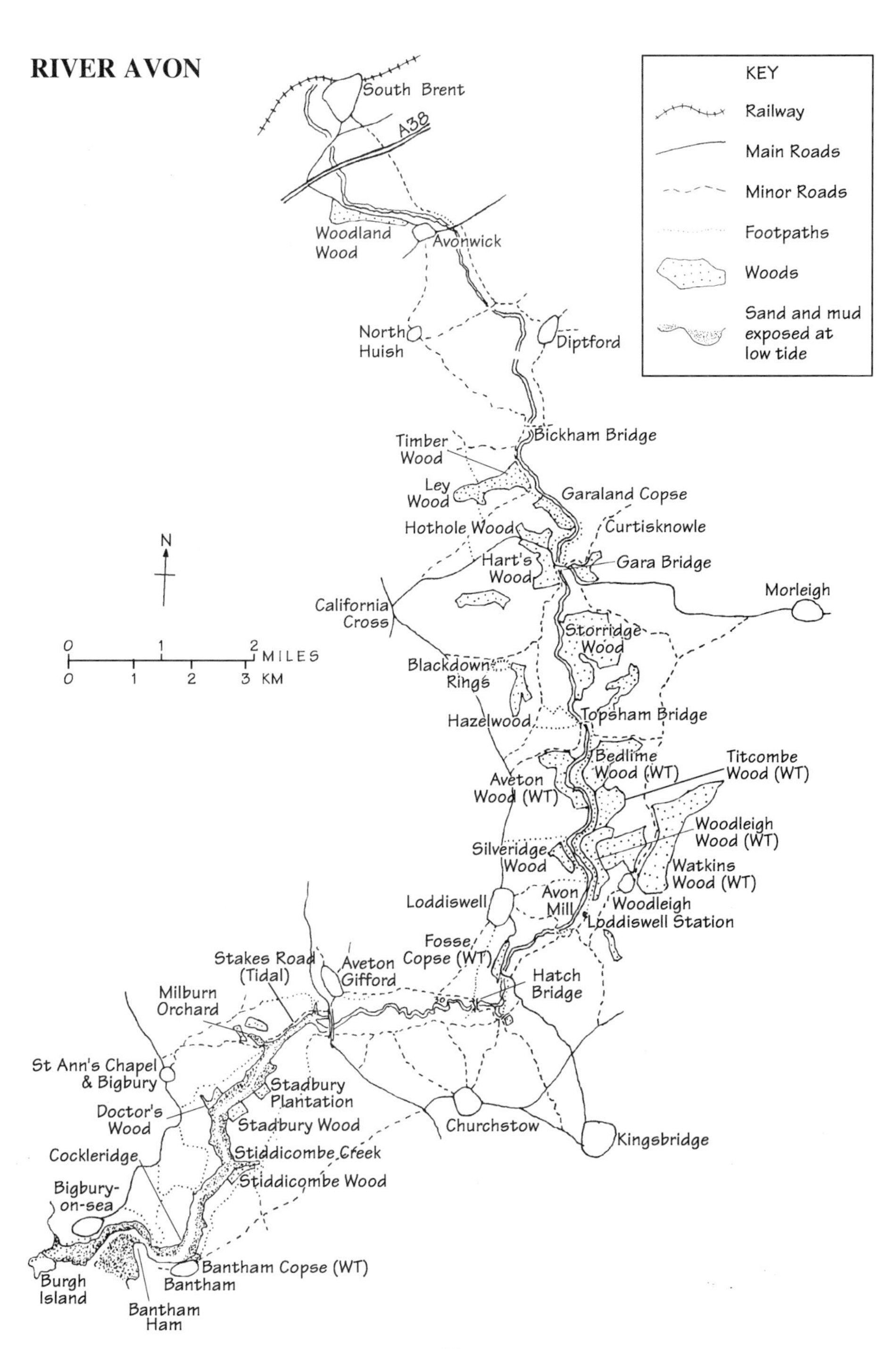
RIVER AVON
KEY
Railway
Main Roads
Minor Roads
Footpaths
Woods
Sand and mud exposed at low tide
N
0 1 2 MILES
0 1 2 3 KM
South Brent
A38
Woodland Wood
Avonwick
North Huish
Diptford
Bickham Bridge
Timber Wood
Ley Wood
Garaland Copse
Hothole Wood
Curtisknowle
Hart's Wood
Gara Bridge
Morleigh
California Cross
Storridge Wood
Blackdown Rings
Hazelwood
Topsham Bridge
Bedlime Wood (WT)
Titcombe Wood (WT)
Aveton Wood (WT)
Woodleigh Wood (WT)
Silveridge Wood
Watkins Wood (WT)
Loddiswell
Avon Mill
Woodleigh
Loddiswell Station
Fosse Copse (WT)
Stakes Road (Tidal)
Aveton Gifford
Hatch Bridge
Milburn Orchard
St Ann's Chapel & Bigbury
Stadbury Plantation
Doctor's Wood
Stadbury Wood
Churchstow
Kingsbridge
Cockleridge
Stiddicombe Creek
Stiddicombe Wood
Bigbury-on-sea
Bantham Copse (WT)
Burgh Island
Bantham
Bantham Ham

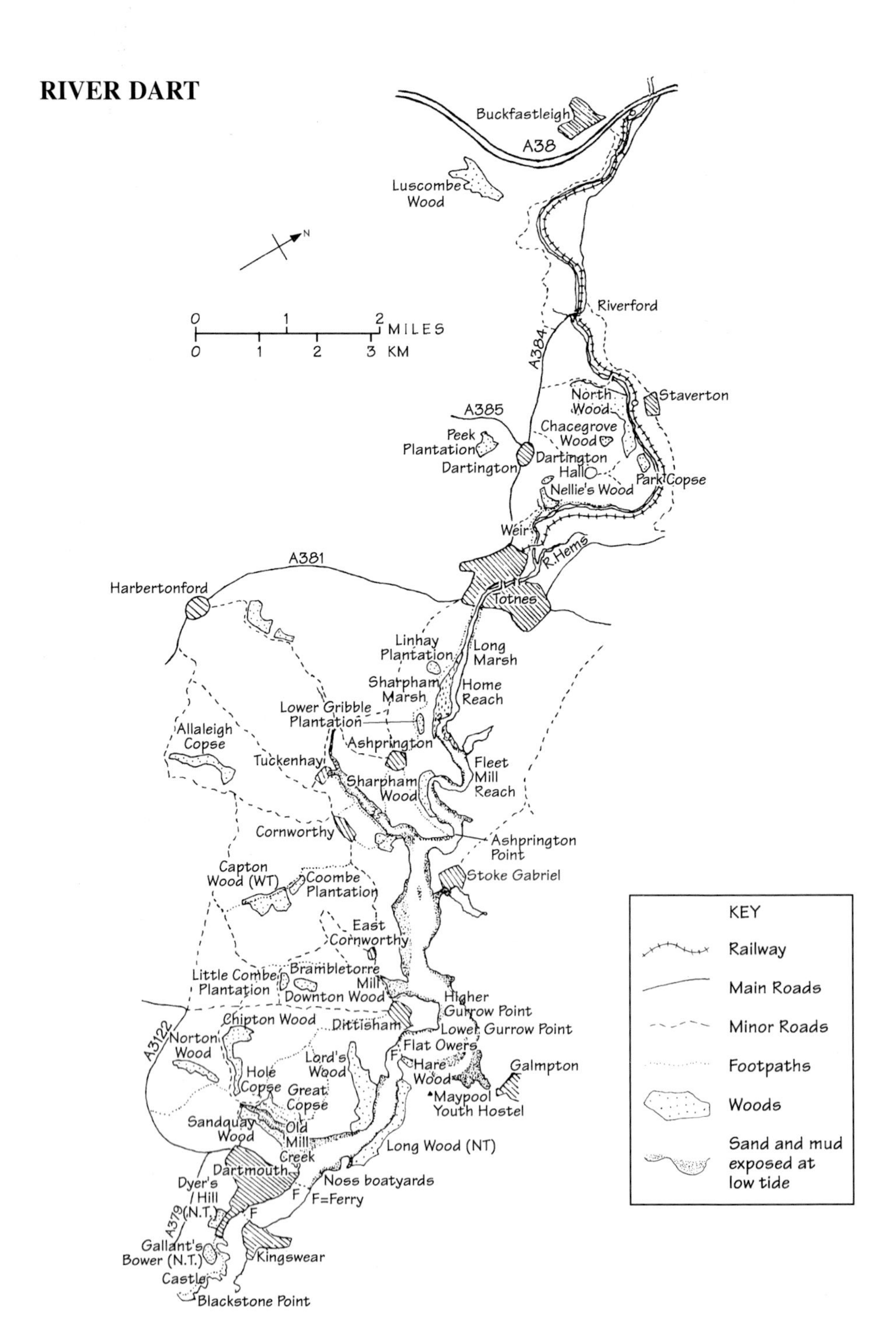
RIVER DART
Buckfastleigh
A38
Luscombe Wood
N
0 1 2 MILES
0 1 2 3 KM
Riverford
A384
A385
Staverton
North Wood
Chacegrove Wood
Peek Plantation
Dartington
Dartington Hall
Park Copse
Nellie's Wood
Weir
R.Hems
A381
Harbertonford
Totnes
Linhay Plantation
Long Marsh
Sharpham Marsh
Home Reach
Lower Gribble Plantation
Allaleigh Copse
Ashprington
Tuckenhay
Fleet Mill Reach
Sharpham Wood
Cornworthy
Ashprington Point
Capton Wood (WT)
Coombe Plantation
Stoke Gabriel
East Cornworthy
Little Combe Plantation
Brambletorre Mill
Downton Wood
Higher Gurrow Point
Chipton Wood
Dittisham
Lower Gurrow Point
A3122
Norton Wood
Flat Owers
Lord's Wood
Hare Wood
Galmpton
Hole Copse
Great Copse
Maypool Youth Hostel
Sandquay Wood
Old Mill Creek
Long Wood (NT)
Dartmouth
Dyer's Hill (N.T.)
Noss boatyards
F=Ferry
A379
Gallant's Bower (N.T.)
Kingswear
Castle
Blackstone Point
KEY
Railway
Main Roads
Minor Roads
Footpaths
Woods
Sand and mud exposed at low tide

III

Woodlands and Heath

Fungi – Boletus species

Woodland was the major habitat of the South Hams before the arrival of man and perhaps it will be again after his departure. Most of the surviving woodlands are in the steep coombes, cleft by the erosion of rivers and streams, but there are fragments throughout the South Hams. There are over two hundred woods, varying in size from the continuous cover along the River Dart, above Holne Bridge, to small copses. Some of the valley woodlands are native oakwoods but most of the woods and copses were originally planted. The oldest established are mostly hard woods but there were many small coniferous plantations – Sitka spruce, Douglas fir, larch – planted after the Second World War. The area around Kingsbridge and Salcombe was described by Rev. John Swete, during his perambulations of Devon in the 1790s, as treeless. He explains that the trees had been felled to supply timber for the thriving shipbuilding industry in the two towns. This part of the South Hams remains relatively bleak and treeless even today.

The maps show the location of most of the woods. Follow the River Yealm from Dendles Wood to Ferry Wood and Brakehill Plantation by the sea. The Erme runs past Piles Copse – a fragment of Dartmoor's ancient woodland – through the Flete Estate woods down to Wonwell beach. The Avon woods stretch from Shipley Bridge to Stiddicombe, with its small heronry overlooking the estuary sands. Names like Garaland Cross, Hothole, Hart's Wood and Storridge, Bedlime, Titcombe, Silveridge and Woodleigh read like romantic names from the Great Western Railway branch line which ran down this valley until 1967. The richest and most extensive woods of the Dart Valley are upstream from Buckfast but other fine woods line its course down to the small National Trust woods of Dyer's Hill and Gallants Bower.

The Gara and the Harbourne both have attractive woods along part of their valleys; few coombes are without at least one copse.

The valley woodlands are usually dominated by oaks but beech, sycamore, ash and sweet chestnut are all common woodland species, with occasional Scots pine and larch. The commonest tree of the forestry plantations is Sitka spruce, with Douglas fir and Japanese larch also frequent species.

It is thanks to the farmers and other private landowners, that many of our woodlands survive and new ones have been planted. Examples of these private woods are seen near Modbury at Butland, Brownston Wood and Ley-Coombe or near Buckland-tout-Saints at Oxen Wood, Bearscombe and Cockshill. In some cases, as at Boreston, near Moreleigh, where Geoff Baines and the late Peter Morris planted a wood, they are open to the public. If you respect and love woodland, you are welcome. Boreston wood has recently been extended. One of the most popular, Millennium projects is to create community woods, as at Chillington and Stokenham, where there is already a young, planted woodland – the Brooking Wood. Valley lakes enhance the idyll below Bedlime Wood.

English Nature manage Yarner Wood, near Bovey Tracey, the Dart Valley Woodlands and Dendles Wood. These are all on the edge of Dartmoor and their typical fauna and flora is described in the chapter on Dartmoor. Following the felling of a coniferous plantation, adjoining Dendles, Dartmoor National Park and English Nature have planned an exciting regeneration project. In addition to their Dart Valley woodlands of Holne and Hembury, Dyer's Hill and Gallants Bower, the National Trust own Halwell, Millbay and Tor Woods by the Kingsbridge estuary, Ferry Wood near Newton Ferrers and the valley wood at Scobbiscombe, near Kingston.

At Slapton the Field Studies Council's reserve officer is responsible for Slapton and France Wood. One can still find evidence of shrapnel embedded in the trees, from the wartime occupation. Permits to visit can be purchased from Slapton Field Centre. The Devon Wildlife Trust manages Lady's Wood, near Wrangaton and Andrew's Wood, near Loddiswell as well as Tod Moor, a small reserve with rushy moor and scrub.

The Woodland Trust woods include the Avon Valley Woods, Aveton, Fosse Copse at Loddiswell, Capton, Penstave and Bantham. The Woodland Trust was founded by a great Devonian conservator, Ken Watkins. He and his wife lived at

Butterbrook, in Harford, and planted fine, mixed woodlands all around their beautiful property. This and the Woodland Trust reserves, scattered all over the country, are a memorial to them. Most are open to the public. Now the Trust have purchased a further 200 acres of arable land next to Avon Woods which will become Watkins Wood in memory of Ken Watkins. This is a very exciting scheme which will take a lifetime to reach maturity, using a mixture of natural regeneration and new plantings.

The trees have a rich flora growing on the trunks and branches. Mosses and lichens wrap themselves round the bark or hang down from the twigs and branches. The mousetail moss, *Isothecium myosuroides*, often grows near the base of the tree trunks. A variety of cypress moss, *Hypnum mammillatum*, which hangs like fine, green hair, is more common higher on the trunks. The common cypress moss, *Hypnum cupressiforme*, often covers old tree stumps and fallen branches. On the twigs and thin branches grow small tufts of moss – *Ulota crispa*. One of the commonest lichens on the tree trunks is *Parmelia caperata*, forming rounded, pale green patches, sometimes as big as a dinner plate. Smaller flakes of silvery grey lichen, with dark undersides, are often *Parmelia perlata*, a lichen sensitive to air pollution and common in the South Hams. From the branches hangs 'oak moss' – not a moss but a powdery grey lichen, in the shape of flexible antlers about two inches long; correctly it is called *Evernia prunastri*. Varieties of *Usnea*, the beard lichens, produce long or tufted grey beards, which also hang from the upper branches. *Usnea articulata*, the sausage lichen, can grow more than a foot long and is seen in most of the Dartmoor woods and those on the higher ridges further south. Ivy may climb up the branches, providing shelter and protection for insects and roosting birds. I have seen a tawny owl roosting, slit-eyed by day, in these thick ivy growths.

Nuthatch.

In the moss, lichen and ivy, and in the crevices of the bark, live a multitude of invertebrates. There are snails, including the trap-door snail – the size and slender shape of a beech bud – springtails, mites, beetles and the larvae and pupae of the smallest moths. These are food for birds, with their specialist feeding techniques. The nuthatches search along and down the branches and trunks. The treecreepers search up the trunk and out and along the branches. Both have long beaks to insert into tufts of moss or crevices of bark. The nuthatch has the strength to also break open hazel nuts. In winter, parties of tits, often joined by treecreepers and goldcrests, forage through the trees. Blue tits are the most common but there are great tits, marsh tits and coal tits and sometimes groups of long-tailed tits. Although these, the 'air gypsies', more often form marauding parties of their own, keeping in touch with their 'syrrup, syrrup' calls. Each species has slightly different techniques for finding food.

In spring and summer, leaf burst is followed by an explosion of bright green leaves on which feed millions of caterpillars. These caterpillars are the staple food for all the birds, from wren to great spotted woodpecker to feed to their young.

In autumn, leaf fall adds another layer to those of the years before. Countless creatures, bacteria and fungi, many too small to see, break down the leaves and each other's bodies to create the rich leaf mould, which nourishes the woodland plants. Robins and blackbirds, great tits and thrushes peck in the leaf litter for food, from snails and the great black slugs to the springtails and little false scorpions. In mid-winter a few woodcock, arrive from Scandinavia, with the redwings and fieldfares. The woodcock probe the leaf litter with their long bills, in the wettest parts of the woods. Their barred plumage of brown and buff gives them perfect camouflage.

The fruits of the trees provide a food source for mammals and birds. In the autumn you often see a jay, with its swooping flight, leaving a wood with an acorn held in its beak. It will eat or bury it, to be recovered later, chance permitting. Under the sweet chestnut trees the silky-lined, spiky, green cases lie split open and squirrels feast on the brown fruits. All our squirrels are grey squirrels. The last red squirrels in the South Hams were near a group of pine trees at Newton Ferrers, where Roger and Philip Hosking filmed them in the 1950s. The smaller, brown beech mast fruits often attract flocks of chaffinches and occasionally their wintering northern cousins, the brambling. Through the hours of darkness, the woodmice eat anything and everything in this harvest festival of the woods, running and leaping like kangaroos over the woodland floor. They hold their long tails aloft and frequently freeze, sensitive whiskers twitching and large black eyes staring, for fear of 'Old Brown', who waits and watches from the branches overhead.

The presence or absence of a shrub layer in a wood has a profound effect on the ground plants that grow there and on the mammal and bird population. Many north-facing woods, which have less light, have a poor shrub layer; the ground flora may be dominated by great wood-rush, as it is at West Alvington Wood, near Kingsbridge, and Ferry Wood at Noss Mayo. Hazel and holly are the most frequent woodland shrubs. Hazel nuts provide food for woodmice, dormice, nuthatches and squirrels. Empty shells that have been split open are the work of squirrels or nuthatches. Mice, usually woodmice, are responsible for those with neat round holes gnawed in them. Those that have a halo of oblique scratches around the hole have been eaten by dormice. Honeysuckle climbs into the hazel bushes and the dormice tear strips off its bark to help make their dome-shaped summer nests. The honeysuckle makes spiral grooves in the hazel stem where it has constricted its growth. In the thick masses of honeysuckle, hanging from the hazel bushes, we have found a goldcrest's nest. The bushes themselves provide more nest sites for birds.

Where the shrub layer is more open, bluebells can flourish. In no other

Dormouse on honeysuckle

country are they as spectacular as in Britain. They spread in broad rivers or lakes of blue, that is not blue and is not purple but some unique 'bluebell-blue' combination. Typical early flowers of the wood include golden saxifrage, which carpets some wet areas by February. Soon after comes dog's mercury, with its insignificant greenish spikes. The foot high stems have alternating pairs of leaves

Wood Sorrel.

at right angles to each other, to trap the most available light. Dog's mercury, with its persistent leaves, creates dark green patches on the woodland floor until winter. Wood anemones are shorter and more delicate, the pink-flushed, white flowers swaying in the April wind. They are scattered through the South Hams. Some woods have none. In others, like Silveridge or Slapton woods, or the riverside entrance to Dartington estate, they are abundant. Every wood has wood sorrel, whose nodding flowers are smaller than the anemones, with fine purple veining on the white petals, and whose shamrock-like, oxalis leaves are bright but pale green. Another early flowerer is moschatel, the town hall clock, which grows on banks in semi-shade. Its single stems are topped by yellow-green flowers with five faces, four looking outwards and one towards the sky. Although more common on shaded hedgebanks, it is particularly prolific in the small copse behind the old school at Brownston. In this same wood, Mr.Wagland acted out

Midsummer Night's Dream, among the bluebells, with his teenage class, in the 1930s.

As the year unfolds new plants follow. Many families of plants have evolved species which are specially adapted for woodland life. There are woodland grasses with attractive, drooping heads: wood mellick, with single-seeded spikelets, the much taller hairy brome, over three feet tall, and the similar giant fescue, which comes into flower a month later, in July. There is wood sedge – small and drooping, wood speedwell – paler than most of our garden speedwells – and yellow pimpernel, which is closely related to the creeping jenny of our rockeries. Wood sanicle is a distinctive woodland umbellifer, with pinkish-white, globular umbels. Our commonest woodland orchid is broad-leaved helleborine, nowhere common but easily overlooked for a slender wood dock. It has a spike of small plum-coloured flowers, which are pollinated by hover-flies.

Enchanter's nightshade is a woodland plant, that spreads effectively by underground runners and tiny stalked burrs, which stick readily to trousers or the coats of dogs, foxes or badgers. It can also be a pernicious garden weed, especially in shady, rambling rectory gardens. The leaves are arranged like those of dog's mercury, adapted for a shady environment. Its reputation for sorcery is reflected in its scientific name – *Circaea* – after Circe, who turned Odysseus' men into pigs!

Occasional burdock plants in woodland are also spread by the same mammals, blundering by. Many of our woods have badgers' setts and foxes' dens. Both may on occasion eat what we would prefer they did not. Foxes' main diet is rabbit, vole and bird. Badgers are omnivores but specialise in worms; a carcase we once sent for analysis was full of them. They also eat tubers, like bluebells, wasp nests and beetles. I have seen beetle elytra in fox and badger droppings.

The robin is by far the commonest woodland bird in our part of Devon. There are about twice as many as the next commonest, the wren. In very cold winters wrens and goldcrests suffer particularly badly and their numbers can be drastically reduced, but within a few years they have usually regained their numbers. It was at Dartington that David Lack did his studies of the robin. One of his discoveries was that many of the female robins in south Devon migrated to France during the winter, leaving the males behind; one of nature's strategies to avoid the worst effects of a hard winter. The chaffinch is usually the next most common woodland bird, with blue tit, wood pigeon, blackbird, great tit, chiffchaff, blackcap, song thrush, nuthatch and goldcrest following after. This order is based on breeding bird censuses I have carried out in the South Hams.

Bryan among the ruins of the old farmhouse in Andrew's Wood.

Most woods also have one or more pairs of tree creeper, marsh tit, coal tit, dunnock, mistle thrush, great spotted woodpecker, cuckoo, crow, magpie, jay, sparrow hawk and buzzard. A wood with a healthy population of predators or parasites, such as these last five species, is a healthy wood. RSPB studies have shown where there is a good population of magpies or other birds of prey, there is a good population of song-birds.

The more varied the habitats in a wood, the greater the variety of wildlife. Where woods have scrub at the edge, or in clearings, there will be long-tailed tits, bullfinches and garden warblers nesting. The edge of a wood is often the most interesting and this edge-effect is increased by having broad rides and clearings within a wood. Then, ground-nesting birds like willow warbler can become very common, using the surrounding trees as singing perches. Tree pipits are attracted to similar habitats round Dartmoor and other higher woods.

Soon after dawn, on a May morning, any wood in the South Hams will have most of these birds singing or calling; defending their territories and attracting a mate. The sound of birdsong and the vision of bluebells beneath dapple-green trees is part of the essence of the South Hams in springtime.

Before leaving the woodland we will visit Andrew's Wood, because this Devon Wildlife Trust nature reserve has woodland and heathy grassland and examples of the succession from one to the other. Ironically the grassland community fits the national vegetation classification M25; Andrew's Wood has a great variety of habitats but nothing like the M25. People come to the South Hams to escape that!

In the 1960s, a teenager, Andrew Walker, spent hours exploring the woods and grassy heath called Stanton Moor. His parents, Colonel and Mrs.Walker, lived in Woolston House and owned Stanton Moor, as well as farmland around Woolston. Andrew found the ruins of an old farmhouse, deep inside the wood and by painstakingly removing piles of rubble, he revealed the lower part of four walls, a fireplace with bread ovens and a flight of stone steps. It was a small mediaeval cottage, with shippen attached and a garden, with star of Bethlehem, monkshood and gooseberry bushes. It had been deserted since about the middle of the Nineteenth Century. Andrew joined the army but whenever he was home on leave he would continue working on the ruins. Then, in 1969 he was killed in a road accident in Germany. His parents sold their house and moved away. The Devon Wildlife Trust were interested in Stanton Moor and the Walker family leased and later sold it to them on one condition: the reserve was to be known not as Stanton Moor but as Andrew's Wood.

Lobelia.

Andrew's Wood is the major site, of only six in Britain, for a rare plant called Heath Lobelia. Devon Wildlife Trust wanted to ensure its survival. For about thirty years they have successfully managed the reserve to encourage the lobelia and a diversity of habitats and wildlife.

The reserve area was a system of fields, divided by Devon banks. The hedgebanks are now cloaked in mosses – fir tree moss, *Polytrichum formosum*, tamarisc moss, *Thudium tamariscinum* and swans neck moss, *Mnium hornum* are the most obvious. Ferns too flourish on the old, shaded banks – broad buckler, with wide, asymmetrical bases to the fronds, hay-scented buckler, with more delicate, parsley-curled fronds, and hard fern, with its stiff spreading fronds around the finer, upright one, which produces the spores. The old hedgerow oaks tower above, now fully-grown specimens, with polypody ferns as well as mosses growing on the branches.

The clearings of heathy grassland, without management, would have become woodland by now. The clearance, by hand, by mechanical cutting and by grazing with cattle or ponies is an unending task. Evidence is there in every clearing of how gorse, birch and sallow seedlings take root, with the occasional oak pushing upwards from its acorn. In three or four years they grow into scrub as tall as a man. Within a decade there is a wood of birch and sallow. Within a century the birches will have died and the climax vegetation of oak forest will have been achieved. All these stages are present in Andrew's Wood.

Each of the grassland clearings are slightly different. The tussocky purple moor grass is dominant in some parts; in others sharp-flowered rush takes over. There are stands of tufted hair grass, a beautiful, tall grass with spreading flowerheads, that look well in a flower display, and thick tussocks of saw-edged leaves. Fine bent is common and the fine-leaved, greyish, bristle bent, which is restricted to moors and heaths of the south and west. Heath grass is present in most of the clearings. Among the grasses are the yellow flowers of tormentil. There are small amounts of all three common heaths – ling, bell heather and cross-leaved heath. More uncommon plants are zig-zag clover, yellow bartsia, saw-wort and devilsbit scabious. For many years there was a population of marsh fritillary butterflies, a nationally declining species, whose caterpillars feed on devilsbit, but they appear to have died out. In the wetter grassland, typical plants are angelica, meadowsweet, bog pimpernel, marsh pennywort and lesser skullcap. In the first clearing, the shaggy red flowers of ragged robin are a fine sight in early summer, with tall pink spikes of marsh orchid. Early purple and heath spotted orchids also grow here. But the plant so many come to see is the lobelia. From a small rosette of bright green, toothed leaves, the stems grow to about eighteen inches. The older plants tend to have more stems, up to about ten, and they can survive about six years. In July and August blue-mauve flowers open on the slender spikes. The flowers have three pointed lower lips, like all the lobelia family. The first two clearings have the largest colonies, sometimes with hundreds of blue-spiked plants within a few yards of each other. Since active management began, in the early 1970s, the number of plants has risen from about 300 to regularly over 2,000, with peaks of nearly 6,000 plants.

Every year the plants are counted. The count is a wonderful, if exhausting, experience. As we move forward, in a line, across the clearings, we disturb hundreds of turquoise leaf-hopper bugs, grasshoppers, butterflies – meadow browns, gatekeepers, marbled whites, skippers, ringlets, tortoiseshell peacocks and painted ladies – and day-flying moths, like the scarlet tiger. Dark, *Pardosa* wolf spiders, run through the grass. Nursery web spiders, with kite-shaped bodies

Lobelia count. L to R: Gordon Waterhouse, Caroline Steele, Ardine Bennett and Natalie Hilton.

and a pale line down their bodies, may run away, holding an egg-sack, like a ping pong ball under their bodies, or wait, with front two pairs of legs outstretched, by a tent like web that protects the young. The male always gives a gift-wrapped fly to the female, to keep her busy, before he attempts the dangerous pleasure of mating. On the gorse bushes and in the tussocky grass, tunnel spiders, *Agelina labyrinthica*, build their sheet-like webs, which shine silver with the early morning dew. For a few weeks in July, male and female actually co-habit amicably in the tunnel at the heart of the web. Around the tunnel are gruesome fragments; a butterfly wing or a grasshopper leg. Once we found a wasp spider, which makes a more conventional web. This is a rare introduced species, which is spreading in southern England.

Children squeal with excitement at the sight of small toads and frogs, lizards basking on the scattered stones or the disappearing tail of an adder.

In some clearings bracken is invasive. It may hide a fox's earth or a badger's sett. I have seen fox cubs playing among the bracken stalks, late in a summer evening. Under the bracken grow violets, the food plant of fritillary butterflies. Small pearl- bordered, dark green and silver-washed fritillaries are present. The silver-washed are the largest of the reserve's butterflies, half flying and half gliding across the clearings. Some of the shrub species we leave in the clearings, the guelder rose, with its cream snowballs of flower and scarlet fruits, and the alder buckthorn, which is the food plant for brimstone butterfly caterpillars. Brimstones are frequent and often the first butterflies we see in the Spring.

Bryan Ashby and Chris Pierce have photographed several birds at the nest in Andrew's Wood. They built a tower hide to watch a great spotted woodpecker. Slightly more accessible was a nuthatch, using one of the nest boxes which we have put up around the reserve. In the usual position, at the top of a bramble thicket, within the wood, they photographed a blackcap's nest. There was a beautiful long-tailed tit's nest in a gorse bush, where three adults were feeding the young. In the grassy clearings they photographed two birds: willow warblers, of which there are about twenty-five pairs in the reserve, and tree pipit. Chris and Bryan had two hides up near a tree pipit's nest. Although the nest was hidden by grass they could see the adults approaching the nest. Suddenly Chris rushed out of his hide; an adder was attacking the nest. He and Bryan attempted to collect the young pipits into the nest, as the adder disappeared into the undergrowth. One of the nestlings had been struck and was dead. The two photographers returned to their hides. Shortly after Chris again rushed from his hide. This time the adder had passed through his hide en route for the nest. The birds scattered and this time Chris and Bryan had learned a lesson; leave nature to take its course. The pipits' instinct to scatter was their best chance of survival. These clearings represent the type of vegetation that would have been commonly used for rough grazing, along the ridges of the South Hams, from the Staddon heights, near Plymouth to the heights above Dartmouth. Place names, like Furzehill and Heathfield, which occurs four times between Yealmpton and Slapton, are evidence of once far more extensive heathlands. Blackdown Rings and the fields around them, which are only a mile from Andrew's Wood, had curlew and nightjar nesting in the 1950s, when Roger Hosking photographed them. It was on these heathy ridges at Stanborough that George Montagu found the nest of a new species of bird, which he called the ashy-coloured falcon and

Great spotted woodpecker at the nest.

we call Montagu's harrier.

In the woodland are all the common species of woodland plants, with common twablade orchid as well as broad-leaved heleborine. It is rich in fungi. On the rotting wood candlesnuff fungus is common. Birch bracket fungus grows from the trunks of the older birches, softening the heart wood, which will then be ideal for the great spotted woodpeckers to excavate their nest. Some of the birches have globular, twiggy growths in the branches. These are possibly caused by an infection of mites and are called, picturesquely, witches' brooms. Under the birch the white spotted, red caps of fly agaric appear in early autumn and under the beech trees purple russulas emerge, pocked white, where the slugs have eaten them. High on the beech trees a shining white fungus – poached-egg fungus – grows. Beneath the oaks, which dominate in the southern part of the wood, some pieces of fallen branch are coloured green. This stain is caused by the green oak fungus and the wood can be used for marquetry. In Andrew's Wood there are examples of most of our native trees, including aspen, which can be identified by sound alone. There is a glade of aspens at the edge of the second clearing. Tall, grey and naked in the winter; in summer they are transformed into spires of shimmering, rustling leaves that "quell or quench the

Fungus foray in Andrew's Wood with Exmoor pony. L to R: Mick Loates, Davis Amas, Gordon Waterhouse, Bob Reed and Josh Hibbard.

Work party in Andrew's Wood. L to R: Frazer Rush, George Watkins, Trevor Appleton, Josh Hibbard, Ann Walker and Bryan Ashby.

leaping sun." – as Gerard Manley Hopkins described them.

There is a reserve guide, which is available in the village shop in Loddiswell. Two circular paths are marked round the reserve, one within the other, winding through clearings and woodland. At any time of the year Andrew's Wood shows woodland and acid grassland land habitats in an evolving mosaic.

If you take the spur path into the south-west corner of the wood, duck under the fallen trunks of oaks brought down in the great storm of 1990, you will find the ruins Andrew Walker exposed. The small farmhouse was probably there when Queen Elizabeth I was Queen. The smell of bread baked in the crumbling ovens, the sound of voices collecting flowers or gooseberries from the garden, the flickering light of oil lamps and candles as the farmer and his wife talk until bedtime and finally the century's decay of thatch and stone – all are present in the air as you stand by Andrew's excavation. As W.B. Yeats wrote, in *He Wishes for the Cloths of Heaven*, "Tread softly, because you tread on (their) dreams".

IV

HEDGEBANK, FIELD AND BY-WAY

Wren

Between the moor, the river valleys and the coast, is the heartland – the patchwork quilt of gentle undulations, cut into by steep coombes. It is partitioned into fields by the Devon hedgebanks of earth and stone. Trees and flowers turn these utilitarian banks into things of beauty and havens for wildlife.

It is only recently that archaeologists have recognised that some of the parallel walls and banks running south from Dartmoor, into these more gentle lands, as at Ugborough, are the continuation of Bronze Age boundaries – reaves. In Bronze Age times, some 4,000 years ago, folk were building permanent hut groups and boundary walls, some of which must be fossilised in our pattern of villages and hedgebanks. Man was already influencing the wildlife around him.

The tracks and lanes follow the edges of the fields, running between two hedges, which may be survivals of prehistoric trackways. Some have wide verges beside them, particularly on the old ridge roads, as above Morleigh and Diptford or between Ugborough and Modbury. Others are sunken between their banks, worn down with age; the hedgerows arch over and, in summer, they become tunnels of green gloom.

Where badgers' or foxes' nightly routes cross a lane, their paths can be seen coming down the hedgerows on either side.

In the revolution of farming methods, since the Second World War, many hedges have been removed to create larger fields. So the hedges that remain are even more important wildlife refuges and corridors along which insects, birds and mammals can travel. They link isolated habitats. The increasing pressures, financial and others, to apply herbicides and pesticides, has led to a reduction of the species along some hedgerows but the hedgerows and verges along our lanes are not treated with weed killers and the most breathtaking visions of our hedgerow flowers are those by our Devon lanes. They lift the spirit of resident and tourist alike.

The Devon hedgebanks are one of our most valuable habitats for wildlife. The number of species of tree in a hedge gives a clue to its age. A study was made of hedges of known age. From this it was found, for example, that a hedge that was about five hundred years old had about five species of tree or shrub in a thirty metre length and a hedge that is about a thousand years old had about ten species in a thirty metre length. So, as a very approximate guide, a hedge may be a hundred years old for every species of tree or shrub in a thirty metre length. Some of the hedges along our parish boundaries have ten species and many have five or more. The most frequently found species are hazel, hawthorn, blackthorn, oak, ash, elder, holly, beech, sycamore, elm, maple, sallow, spindle and dogwood.

One of the delights on a February day is to see the female flowers of the hazel, opening like tiny red spiders from the fat buds, while the male flowers, long yellow lambs' tails, hang in their thousands. In the autumn the squirrels and mice feast on the nuts. Dormice nest in the thicker hedges. The berries of hawthorn and holly attract the flocks of redwing and other thrushes. Elderberries and blackberries are eaten by our resident birds and the summer warblers. The jays come for the oak's acorns and the chaffinches gather under the beech hedge to peck where the beechmast has fallen. But the hedgerow trees and bushes can only fruit where they are not cut annually. Cutting in a rotation of a few years and leaving occasional bushes to grow to full size, greatly increases the attractiveness and wildlife value of a hedge. Few elms ever grow to maturity now, after the arrival of Dutch elm disease, but suckering lines of hedgerow elms can be everlasting, sending up new suckers after each attack has killed the new growth. Lines of rather stunted but mature trees survive particularly well by the coast, south and east of Kingsbridge.

The flowers of the hedgebank and grass verge make a continuous display throughout the year. Winter heliotrope, a garden escape, is spreading along many roadside banks. The pink-mauve flower spikes are out all through January, smelling of vanilla. The new leaves follow – large, kidney shaped and overlapping to shade out other plants. Along some hedges, there are patches of green-veined, nodding snowdrops, spearing up through the creeping ivy early in the new year.

By February the golden stars of lesser celandine shine out, particularly on south-facing hedgebanks, sometimes in a continuous golden dazzle. They are wonderfully various. I have found flowers with from seven to fourteen petals and the small, shovel-shaped leaves may have white blotches or black blotches or no blotches at all. In May they shrivel away and are invisible till the next year.

The insignificant green flower spikes of dog's mercury – male and female on separate plants – open in February, above the dark- leafed stems.

Thrum-Eyed Primrose, with stamens uppermost.

Pin-eyed Primrose, with stigma uppermost.

The primrose flowers from before Christmas and in all kinds of habitats, but it is in March and on the hedgebanks that it looks best. The pale cream flowers, in clusters, make splashes of pure colour against the dark banks and are nowhere more beautiful than in the South Hams.

In the open, along the grassy verges at the foot of the banks, dandelions make a ribbon of yellow, later to turn grey as the dandelion clocks develop into smoky globes. A month later, the dandelion's tall relative, beaked hawksbeard, with red-veined stems and dandelion flowers, lines the verges.

On slightly shaded banks, pale green and insignificant stems and fingered leaves of town hall clock grow; its scientific name of *Adoxa* means 'lacking in glory'. Also hiding their glories are the sweet violets, their deep, velvet blue flowers at least half hidden beneath the dull, heart-shaped leaves.

Before the end of the month, the first umbellifer, Alexanders, is in flower. It seldom grows further than about five miles from the sea. Along many hedges and verges its shining, celery-like leaves have been growing all winter and, near the sea, make an almost continuous cover, but only now do the tall umbels of yellow-green blossom open. Their sickly scent attracts the black St. Mark's flies, which emerge around 25th March – his saint's day. By late summer, the only signs of it are the bleached stems and clusters of black seeds.

The end of March is also the time of blackthorn winter, when the blackthorn blossom smothers the dark, spiky twigs, as if with snow. When the March winds blow, they whip a blizzard of snowflake petals from the hedges.

By April and into May a host of flowers are following each other as leading characters in a floral tableau. Especially common in the South Hams is the early purple orchid. The orchids cluster in groups along the grassy verges and hedgebanks, their purple spires rising from black-blotched leaves. Jack-by-the-hedge shoots upwards to nearly three feet, before bursting into little white flowers. The orange-tip and green-veined white butterflies lay their eggs on it or upon

Orange Tip on Cuckoo flower or Ladies Smock.

the cuckoo flower. Red, white and blue become the patriotic colours of the hedgerow. The pinkish-red is red campion, the white is greater stitchwort and ramsons and the blue is made by drifts of bluebells, tall clumps of green alkanet and humble, birdseye speedwell. Many people mistake the ramsons, or wild garlic, for lily of the valley. The leaves are similar but the flower is a white globe and the smell of garlic is overpowering. Like the bluebells, the ramsons and the pinky-red campion can create almost solid washes of colour.

The characteristic hedgerow grass of the early spring is sweet vernal grass, short and simple headed but with the scent of hay fields.

Above: Yellow Archangel – a plant of old woodland and hedgerow.

Below: Barstard Balm, a rare speciality of our South Hams' hedgerows.

Spiking up through the growing herbage are the pointed cowls of cuckoo pint. Pint is an Anglo-Saxon term for penis. Tiny owl midges are attracted by the scent of the purple, penis-shaped spadix. They are trapped overnight in the cavity beneath it and pollinate the embryo seeds with pollen.

It has other, more respectable but interesting names, such as wild arum, parson-in-the-pulpit, lords and ladies, hobblegobbles and kittycomedown-thelanejumpupandkissme!

A month later its relative, the rare cuckoo pint, comes into flower. This grows by sheltered hedgebanks near the sea, such as at South Milton or Thurlestone. It is taller and the pointed cowl droops at the top. It always has a yellow spadix, whereas the common species only occasionally has a yellow spadix. The best time to locate the rare cuckoo pint is in October and November, when the paler-veined, arrow-shaped leaves shoot up two months earlier than those of common cuckoo pint.

Sorrel, with its thin, red spires, is an elegant dock, flowering in May. It is a food plant for the small copper butterfly. Goosegrass, climbs up the hedge, its weak stems covered in lines of minute hooks that cling, like velcro, to every twig and leaf it passes; cleavers is its other name. Soon the almost invisible flowers turn to little round burrs of fruit – the tiny sticky-buds or sweethearts, that the children throw at each other. Round black beetles feed on the whorls of goosegrass leaves. They are called bloody-nose beetles from their habit of extruding blood from their mouth, when molested.

Much less common, is crosswort, a yellow flowered relative of goosegrass, which is also a hedgerow plant. Common violets rise on slender stalks from shining heart-shaped leaves, on which the dark green and small pearl-bordered fritillary butterflies feed. Along damper, shaded hedges, the gold and orange-veined dead- nettle flowers of yellow archangel shine through their leaves.

Towering above the others, cow parsley makes a frothy edge to many hedges and roadsides; in some parts it is called Queen Anne's lace. Perhaps this is the best-known of all the umbellifers. In grassy, slightly shaded hedgebanks, another very small relation, called pignut grows. It has delicate umbels and very finely divided leaves; from its roots grow nutty tubers.

The balm-leaved figwort is especially successful around Kingsbridge, although there is a small clump as far north as by the road bridge at Cornwood. It thrives where hedge banks have been disturbed, by a landslip or close cutting by the hedge-cutter. The maroon and yellow coloured flowers are pollinated by wasps, which you will see weaving round the tall plants. They grow to about four feet high. Their leaves are broad and wrinkled, like balm. We find two others of the family – common and water figwort. All are food plants for the little black and white weevils, called figwort weevils. Sometimes on the figworts you also find mullein moth caterpillars. These white caterpillars, with yellow and black spots and marks, usually feed on mullein. Mullein, scientifically called *Verbascum*, also grows up in May, on hedgebanks and in waste places. It has yellow flowers on a stout, felty-grey stem and foxglove-like leaves that are often in holes and tatters, on account of those caterpillars.

Many cranesbills, the wild geraniums, grow in hedges. The tallest is the purple-pink Pyrenean cranesbill, the smallest is the common dovesfoot cranesbill and my favourite is the long stalked cranesbill, *Geraniuma columbinum*, with its drooping flowers like pink-breasted doves. Where the banks are more stony, the shining cranesbill grows. This and the less common, round- leaved cranesbill are the two species that do not have notches in the ends of their five, rounded petals. In most hedgebanks herb robert will grow – the commonest of the cranesbills.

From May, through June and into July the white, golden-centred ox-eye daisies, or marguerites, make the grass verges along the roads a picture of white and gold. It is less common as a traditional hay meadow flower but still flourishes on the drier, grassy hedgebanks.

On the driest, stony banks and on walls through every village, the red valerian, a naturalised plant from the Mediterranean, is completely at home. Its masses of pink or red, or sometimes white, blossom is eye-catching. Sometimes you see a humming-bird hawk moth, hovering, just like a tropical bird, taking its nectar through its long tongue. Along the damper banks, and especially in the north of the South Hams, the elegant and tall common valerian grows. Its flower heads are a delicate pink shade of white. It is more refined and much less common than the red valerian.

As the Alexanders and the cow parsley fade away, new, hairy umbellifers replace them. The small hairy one is rough chervil, whose umbels droop in bud. The big hairy one is hogweed, which dominates the hedges in mid-summer. In some hedges there are stands of an equally tall but slender umbellifer, hairless and with purple blotches on the stem. This is the deadly poisonous hemlock.

By June the towering spikes of foxgloves dominate the hedgerow. Bumblebees struggle into the thimble-flowers for their nectar and pollinate them. Almost hidden, lower in the undergrowth, the finer-petalled flowers of lesser stitchwort have replaced the white shirt buttons of greater stitchwort. June is the month when the hedgerow vetches are at their best. The dusky purple flowers of bush vetch have been out since April but now the common vetch, with purple or pink flowers, the diminutive hairy and slender tares and the yellow flowers of meadow pea all struggle up the hedgebanks. The most attractive of the vetches is the tufted vetch. The tangled stems clamber over the hedges and are festooned with purple-blue spikes of flower. Along the roadside from Staverton to Buckfastleigh they are particularly fine.

High above the hedgerow plants, champagne time has arrived. The elder bushes are smothered in bunches of creamy blossom, as big as tea plates. The dominant grass is now false oat-grass, its plumes protruding above the hedgerow flowers.

In July the heavy scent of honeysuckle blossom is in the air. Its stems have climbed over the hedges and up the trees and telegraph poles and they are all hung with curling cream blossoms. A small cream coloured crab spider, with

Honeysuckle and Crab Spider.

dimples in its abdomen identical to those on the petals of the honeysuckle, lies in wait for the insects attracted by the scent. The flowers continue into autumn, mixed increasingly with the clusters of green and red, poisonous berries.

This is the month when the hedge bedstraw covers the hedges in veils of white, made up of thousands of tiny white crosses. It belongs to the same family as goosegrass and is also a food plant for the bloody-nose beetles. Meadowsweet's candyfloss flowers on cherry-red stems, are very common by the damper hedgerows and ditches. This is another plant where crab spiders wait for the insects, attracted by the honeyed scent.

The mauve flower-heads of scabious and the purple of knapweed appear and continue for most of the summer. Nearer the coast, there is also greater knapweed, related to hardheads but with larger and more rayed flowers.

Many members of the mint family flower in July. The creeping ground ivy is out from early spring. The rare bastard balm blooms in May and June, scattered thinly over the southern half of the area. The best place to find it is along a lane that leads northwards from Churchstow. In June the hedge woundwort and the stinking black horehound bloom but it is in July that the burgundy-pink clumps of marjoram appear, the paler common calamint, and creamy-white wood-sage. For me, the most attractive of the family is betony. At a glance you could mistake it for a patch of bell heather, the red-purple is so intense. Close to, you could be looking at an orchid, the spikes are so tall and dense-flowered. It is a frequent plant but there is an especially fine stand along the bank at Borough Farm, where the Kingsbridge Show is held. Sometimes, with the betony, on shaded banks, are three yellow flowers of different families: the beautiful St. John's wort, leafy hawkweed and golden-rod.

With August, in mid-summer, comes the first feeling of autumn in the hedgerows. There is the last of the umbellifers, the burnet saxifrage. The pale yellow of toadflax and the deep yellow of fleabane, which continue till the frosts. Hemp agrimony, beloved of butterflies, opens its pink-grey, mop-head flowers. Nearly as tall as the hemp agrimony is the silvery leaved, aromatic mugwort.

Throughout the summer the round, fleshy leaves of wall pennywort persist in banks and walls, their cream flowers briefly rising on slender spikes and withering away. The ferns too are there all summer. The black spleenwort is small, with a black base to its stem. Bracken is the tallest fern, dominating some lengths of hedgerow. The Americans call it eagle fern, because of the pairs of wide based fronds ascending the stem, like wings. The commonest fern in the hedges is soft shield fern. Male fern is frequent, usually the golden-scaled species. Polypody, grows on banks as well as on walls and up trees. On shaded and wetter banks, broad buckler and lady fern are more frequent.

In autumn, the blackberries ripen and the ivy flowers open. Crowds of insects – bees, hover flies, drone flies and butterflies gather to feast on the last food sources of the year. Coiled vines of black bryony are hung with berries, which turn from green to gold to red.

This is the floral backdrop within and around which the animals live. The hedges are the reservoirs from which the insects and small mammals can spread into the fields and the highways by which they can travel from one area to another.

There are scores of insects. One of the first you see, in March, is the holly blue butterfly, which lays its first eggs on holly. You may see it flickering, pale blue around a holly bush. Later in the year, the next generation lays its eggs more often on ivy. Bumble bees make their mossy, underground nests in holes in the hedgebank. Click-beetles, irridescent green, thick-knee beetles, weevils and leaf-hoppers climb up the early summer leaves. Ladybirds, especially seven-spots, both adults and larvae, set to work on eating the aphids that swarm on the red campion and the stinging nettles. The frothy cuckoo spit, spattered over the vegetation, hides the soft frog-hopper insects within. As summer progresses there are more scorpion flies, with curved abdomens, shield bugs and other plant bugs. With the orange-tips and the green-veined whites come the tortoiseshells and peacock butterflies. By July the gatekeeper butterflies are fluttering around the bramble blossom by every gateway. The dark bush crickets, the females with ovipositors like Saracen scimitars, have grown two inches long and are singing their scraped songs day and night. All year long the caterpillars of moths and butterflies nibble away at their various food plants, in a livery of camouflage or warning colours against the winged predators. Some larvae feed from within, like the golden pigmy moth, whose larvae make the white scribble mines on the leaves of brambles. Many larvae will have parasites inside them, the larvae of ichneumon flies. By their rapidly vibrating antennae, the ichneumons search out caterpillars and lay their own eggs inside them, using their ovipositor needles. In autumn the daddylonglegs craneflies blunder into the beautiful orb webs of the garden cross spiders. Long-legged harvestmen walk through the leaves and wasps and red admiral butterflies swarm round the ivy blossom.

Gatekeeper.

These and many more are food for the insectivorous birds. In every season, the robin, the wren and the dunnock creep through the hedge picking up unconsidered trifles. The blackbird and the scarcer song thrush, find berries and snails. The blue tit, the great tit, the long-tailed tit and the goldcrest make regular forays along the hedgerows, searching for invertebrates. The tits will peck open the marble galls on the oaks, to eat the soft gall-wasp grub within. Chaffinches, greenfinches and goldfinches, the more secretive bullfinches and gangs of sparrows not only feed in the hedge but use it as a refuge, a vantage point and a protected highway, from which to make forays to feed in the fields and other habitats. Yellowhammers and, near the coast the rare cirl buntings do the same, often looking out from a topmost twig along the hedge. In the winter redwings and fieldfares and other thrushes use the hedges, eating the hips, haws and holly berries. Sparrow hawks are masters of the hedgerow attack. They fly low down one side of a hedge, quickly flip over the hedge and descend on a flock of feeding or sheltering birds on the other side. They often appear in front of your car, flying down a lane, low over the tarmac, and suddenly sideslip over the hedgebank

In summer all the resident species may use the hedgerow as a nest site. Then the magpies, crows and jays will scan the hedges for nests, which they can rob; any nest will do. The cuckoo, which has become more scarce, will particularly look for dunnocks' nests in which to lay an egg of her own.

Chiffchaffs, when they arrive in March, often sing first from a hedgerow, they may nest at the base of the hedge and skulk through its branches on migration. Those that remain through the winter in the South Hams, rely on hedges for shelter and food.

The summer visitor that is the true warbler of the hedgerow, is the whitethroat, or nettlecreeper. When the males arrive in late April they immediately announce their arrival by singing from the top of the hedge, head held high, revealing the spiky-feathered white throat. They may take flight, still singing, tail rocking in the air, until they land back on the hedge; a scratchy, disjointed song, evocative of hedgerow-summer.

Between sheltered hedgerows and through "tunnels of green gloom" where the lanes wind, swallows swoop low over the tarmac, hawking for insects.

Tarmacadam has brought a revolutionary change to the South Hams' network of tracks and routeways; no more muddy tracks in winter and dusty, rutted ones in summer. There have been other new routes which have brought verges and embankments of a different nature.

The railway from South Brent to Kingsbridge was opened in 1893. This may have introduced Oxford ragwort, which occurs on waste ground at South Brent and Kingsbridge. The railway network spread its thistle-down seeds all over the country; before that, it only grew on walls in Oxford. Primroses, ox-eye daisies, early purple, marsh and common spotted orchids and a succession of other meadow flowers, through the seasons, grew along the cuttings and embankments. In 1967 the line was closed and in just over thirty years thickets of ash and sycamore have grown to maturity and, beneath them thrive ferns, mosses and woodland flowers. The path, by the old railway line, from Loddiswell station to Topsham Bridge is particularly attractive.

In the 1970s the A38 was transformed into a dual carriageway, making a scar across the land. Now its verges have matured and are as wildlife friendly as the railway cuttings used to be.

They have a similar variety of rich grass and scrubland habitats. Kestrels hover over the verges to pounce on the voles that burrow through the grasses.

Topsham Bridge.

The slipstream of passing vehicles has brought many plant seeds, including Oxford ragwort. In March, parts of the central reservation and verges are pale lilac and white, as if salt had been sprinkled. These are the flowers of early scurvy-grass and some of the taller, white, common scurvy-grass – both salt-marsh plants. Their seeds have been spread from where motorways cross estuaries. Because we grit our motorways with salt, during the winter, the scurvy-grass seeds have responded, germinated and thrive in their new habitat; saltmarsh by the motorway.

The Aveton Gifford by-pass also brought a spectacular flowering. In the early 1990s, the verges were ablaze with red corn poppy flowers and ox-eye daisies. All they needed was disturbance to wake the seeds, which had lain dormant.

The fields make up the coloured patches of the undulating quilt, that is the heartland of the South Hams. The hedges surround them and most of the tracks and lanes respect their boundaries. The fields of the undulating plateau are very different from those of the steep coombes. Most of the arable fields are on the plateau; cereals, rape, flax, grass leys for silage and a little hay. Any pasture fields are likely to be improved and resown. On the steep slopes of the coombes are the permanent pastures, some of them ancient, with a beautiful diversity of meadow flowers; sheep and cattle are grazed. Patches of gorse and other scrub are frequent, with copses and valley woods.

From these fields the farmers make their livings, and have done for many centuries. It is easy to find fault with farmers. Their impact on the countryside is so obvious to the eye. But they are under more pressures than most. They have had a hand in making virtually all the habitats that produce the diversity of wildlife of the South Hams. Some of the developments in farming practices have reduced diversity but the farmer, like us all, is carried along on the tide of 'progress'. The men and women in the farming industry are the human heart of the South Hams. We can help them, in difficult times, by valuing their role, respecting their land and keeping to the country code.

Wherever there is a trampled and tractor-worn gateway into a field there will be pineapple weed and usually knotgrass and wayside cudweed. Around the edges of the arable fields we still see some of the weeds, which were common in the days of the horse: field pansies, field madder, a few poppies, field woundwort, little cresses, like lesser swine-cress and penny-cress and the trailing stems of black bindweed. The small-flowered buttercup, nationally a scarce plant, is quite common as an arable weed here. Sharp-leaved fluellen is a pretty, trailing weed, with two coloured, yellow and maroon, snapdragon flowers. The semi-parasitic, red bartsia is frequent. Sun and petty spurge are common but the little, dwarf spurge has become rare. The Venus' looking glass, grew round the edge of one arable field, until a few years ago. It is now thought to be extinct in Devon but I suspect the seeds are still there, dormant.

Set-aside and the more sensible, long-term strategy of countryside stewardship schemes, give an opportunity for some of the more attractive arable weeds to reappear. An ideal compromise is to leave a fallow or untreated margin around the edges of fields. It is there that important and beneficial insects, such as grasshoppers, caterpillars and ladybirds can spread. They are key links in the food chains that support the declining farm birds.

Schemes such as this have brought the cirl bunting back from the edge of extinction as a British breeding bird.

The insects and the weed seeds are food for skylarks, yellowhammers, chaffinches, linnets, greenfinches and goldfinches, that all feed round the edges of these fields of the arable plateau. Skylarks and yellowhammers are typical birds of the plateau, Both are declining in numbers, nationally. Skylarks have suffered a drastic reduction in the last twenty years. Where there is encouragement to leave winter stubbles, there is an immediate bonus for wildlife. In the recent survey of wintering skylarks, flocks of over fifty were common on winter stubble fields, elsewhere there were very few. Yellowhammers, finches and meadow pipits, that have moved down from the moor during the winter, were also in good numbers on the stubble.

In summer the breeding skylarks do best in fields of spring cereals, rather than the normally more economic winter planting. The whitethroats are far more common round the plateau fields than down in the coombes. Their numbers plummetted in the 1970s as a result of the droughts in sub-Saharan Africa, but have recovered; hopefully a good omen for our declining birds. The sound of whitethroats and yellowhammers in the hedges and skylarks reeling out their song from the skies, is the essence of Maytime on our farming heartland.

Many other birds come to glean in the fields. Wood pigeons, rooks and their cousins the jackdaws come, sometimes in clouds, to peck for grain or prod for wireworms. Wintering flocks of starlings, with their finer beaks, feed on other invertebrates in the grass and topsoil. The dung spreader provides an attraction. After a field has been spread, rooks, jackdaws, magpies and starlings may descend, picking up the juicy morsels. Magpies and jackdaws sit on the backs of cattle and sheep, acting as nit nurses. Pheasants are very common pecking for seeds round the edges of fields but partridges are virtually a bird of the past. The Game Conservancy's research blames the reduction of weed seeds and cover around the edge of fields, for their decline.

In winter on traditional sites, such as Stanborough, Chuchstow and St. Ann's Chapel, the plateau fields are feeding and roosting sites for flocks of golden plover and lapwing. They come to pasture and freshly ploughed fields. There they are joined by gulls, which still follow the plough as they did when the horses were pulling it, half a century ago. Black-headed gulls are the most common, with herring gulls and, in winter, numbers of the green-legged, common gulls. In spring herring gulls become much more common; these are the only gulls that commonly stay with us to nest along the cliffs. In spring also migrating wheatear, often stop on the ploughed fields, perched upright, grey or fawn, feeding on insects. A scarce denizen of the fields is the March-dancing hare.

Buzzards follow the plough, harrow and combine. They walk over the furrows, with an ungainly gait, like a farmyard hen, snatching worms, beetles, moles and voles – anything that moves. The buzzard could be the emblem of the South Hams.

Whitethroat.

Down in the coombes the buzzard nests, in tall trees in the hedgerows or copses and woodland. It floats in the sky, over the valleys, spiralling on thermals or rocking on its wings on a blustery day, looking especially for rabbits. The rabbits' burrows are on the steep grassy slopes and under the gorse thickets.

These valley pastures, where sheep and cattle roam, are also home to fox and badger. The badgers scratch up hundreds of worms from the dewy pasture and scrabble for bluebell bulbs and pignut. Elder bushes often flourish round their setts. Elder is rich in mosses and most elders have some Judas' ears hanging from them. They are greyish-fawn fungi, with the shape and the texture of a human ear; apparently they are edible!

The foxes prey on the rabbits, that have increased in numbers, even though myxomatosis still recurs. They also search out the after-birth after lambing; they are less likely to prey on the lambs themselves. The coombes are very much the fox's habitat and you often meet with one early in the morning. He will stand still, eye you coolly, perhaps twitch a white-tipped tail, and then, with nonchalance, walk away.

The pastures have meadow, creeping and bulbous buttercups and many of the dandelion family: catsear and hawkbits. On drier mounds, mouse-ear hawkweed grows, with hairy leaves, white-backed and silky to the touch. Daisies, dandelions and the tiny eyebright are all common in the short grass. Recently a Mediterranean species of tongue orchid has been found growing in old grassland; a sign of warmer climate?

The older the grassland, the more species of grass it has. Following the sweet vernal grass, come crested dogstail and meadow foxtail. Rough meadow-grass, cocksfoot, Yorkshire fog and Timothy are common and the perennial rye-grass. In well-drained soil, are soft brome and red fescue, with its fine leaves. Around the bramble patches and the hedges, false oat-grass often dominates. As the summer holidays arrive, the most delicate grasses, the fine and creeping bents, come into flower.

Amongst the grasses live the click-beetles, whose wire-worm larvae eat the grass roots. The grasshoppers, field and meadow, can be abundant and a host of plant-sucking, leaf-hopping insects. On the well-drained, drier slopes ants thrive and their ant-hills make tummocks in the pasture.

There are a multitude of beetles, including those who lay their eggs in or under cow-pats: the black dung beetles and the red and black carrion beetles. Glow-worms may emerge, on short grass by stony banks, preying on the banded and garden snails.

The khaki-coloured dung flies are present nearly the whole year through, sat upon the faeces. There can be eight million spiders in an acre of natural grassland, trapping and chasing the unwary insects.

This rich supply of insects feeds the birds and their nestlings. The gorse, scrub, and tufted grasses provide the nest sites. The combes are the best places to find a green woodpecker, which feeds on the ants in the sloping pasture fields. It nests in the woodland – excavating holes in old trees, like its more common relation, the great-spotted woodpecker. The lesser-spotted woodpecker is much less common but it too can be seen in the narrow coombes, nesting usually by a stream, in an old, rotten alder. Both yellowhammers and groups of linnets frequently nest in gorse. This is also favoured by long-tailed tits, as a nest site. Thick scrub provides nest sites for all the common hedgerow birds and is favoured by the pink-breasted, white rumped bullfinch. In winter, areas of scrub are often used by redwings as night-time roosts.

All the warblers, except the whitethroat, are more common around the pasture fields of the combes, by the scrub, woods and copses. The blackcaps nest in the top of the blackberry clumps. The chiffchaffs nest in grass, often at the base of bramble clumps, or a few inches to a foot above the ground. The willow warblers nearly always nest on the ground in tussocky grass. The garden warblers are the least common and are birds of the scrubland.

The advent of the JCB has enabled farmers to move mountains and work miracles. One of the positive changes for wildlife has been the proliferation of ponds and small lakes. With piped water to cattle-troughs and the end of horsepower on the farm, many old ponds had silted up, There is now a new generation of ponds with moorhen, mallard and the ever more successful Canada goose nesting by them. Some even have coots.

The farm quarries, which provided stone for our South Hams, farms, villages and churches, have fallen into disuse. Some have been used for landfill. A few of the larger ones have jackdaw, kestrel and raven nesting. Even the majestic, peregrine falcon sometimes nests in old quarries, where they are private and inaccessible.

When exploring the hedges and farmland, please respect privacy and keep to the lanes and public footpaths.

Long-tailed Tit removing a faecal sac from its nest.

V

VILLAGE AND FARM

Swifts

Most of the people of the South Hams live in the small towns and villages and in and around the farms. A community of plants and animals has developed, living alongside man, because of or in spite of him.

Through the Bronze and Iron Ages, the size of settlements grew. By 1000BC the Iron Age hill forts at Brent Hill and along the heathland ridges at Norton, Capton, Stanborough and Blackdown, may mark the first areas of major forest clearance and the creation of centres of population. The Romans reinforced permanent settlements during the four hundred years they were masters of Celtic Britain. With their system of roads and increased trade, plants and animals arrived and spread round the country, from port, to inland town and from village to village.

By about 700 AD the Saxon invaders and settlers were taking over the Iron Age, Celtic settlements and making them their own. They gave them names ending in 'ton' or 'ham' e.g. Kingston, Stokenham.

The Saxon metaphor, which describes human life – like a sparrow that enters a banqueting hall, flies its length and then departs – shows that the house sparrow lived with them in their villages. The sparrow, the robin and the wren, the finches, the blackbirds and the swallows are homely birds that our Saxon ancestors would have known well. The Celts, the Welshmen or 'Wallas' as the Saxons called them, either inter-married or moved up to the poorer lands; any name including 'Walla' marks a Celtic settlement. Moreleigh and Wallaton Cross must have been more isolated then than now. The wilder birds of heath and moor – the curlew, the golden plover, the meadow pipit, the raven – may have been the birds the outcast Celts heard.

After the Norman conquest in 1066, earth and wooden forts were built to create fear. The remnants of the motte and bailey castle within Blackdown Rings, near Loddiswell, still stand. On frosty winter mornings, I have disturbed woodcock, from its ditch. The Totnes castle was made more permanent by a stone shell-keep, below which the townspeople of Totnes lived in cowed obedience. The greatest legacy the Normans have left us are the churches, standing proudly in almost every village. Although established by the Saxons, most were built or rebuilt of stone by the Normans, to be restored and altered for a thousand years, through the mediaeval period to Victorian times and the present.

As Norman authority brought stability, in mediaeval and Tudor ages farmers and the richer gentry built more substantial houses, both in the towns and villages and out on the farms. Some old South Hams farm houses, still in use today, have timbers in their roofs which were felled in the fourteenth century. Shippens for the animals, threshing and storage barns, courtyards and galleries, thatched and slated roofs all provided lodging and food supplies for birds and other animals, great and small.

In Tudor times, Walter Raleigh and Francis Drake, as boys, may have visited relatives in their fine houses at Modbury and Hatch Arundell. Did they see a barn owl leaving the barn at Hatch, before dusk, and flying, ghost-like, over the hay meadows? Did they, like us, play by the River Avon, at Hatch Bridge and see the dipper and the kingfisher shoot beneath it?

The shipbuilding industry, of the eighteenth and nineteenth centuries, which left the countryside round Kingsbridge and Salcombe treeless, may have been responsible for bringing balm-leaved figwort to the South Hams. Our schooners brought citrus fruits from the Azores and Mediterranean countries, where the figwort is common. We, with areas round a few ports in Cornwall and Wales, are the stronghold for this rare plant, especially in and around the coastal towns and villages.

In the nineteenth and twentieth centuries our villages have expanded dramatically. Housing has spread around the old centres, like a fairy ring, but more obtrusively. There are terraces of Victorian and Edwardian houses, semi-detached houses from between the wars, post-war Cornish units. The modern estates tend to be on the edges of the communities; in some cases, as in Ivybridge, dwarfing the earlier settlement.

On 'waste' land, around the farm buildings, where the soil is often disturbed, there are interesting plants. The tall mulleins are at home here. So are clumps of burdock, with the big, sticky burrs, which children throw at each other. The large bindweeds, with big, white trumpets of flower, clamber over the weedy patches. Black nightshade is common; a low growing weed with white flowers, rather like a potato's, and green berries which turn black. Fathen, used as spinach in prehistoric times, smothers freshly bulldozed banks. Where chicken have been kept in the past, disturbance like this may activate seeds of the rare alien, thorn-apple, whose pale violet trumpet flowers develop into spiny fruits, like an elongated conker case. This South American plant was probably introduced with imported chicken feed, much earlier in this century.

Where there are frequently trodden paths around the farm, pineapple weed, knotgrass, wayside cudweed and ratstail plantain will thrive.

Farms have always attracted birds. Gangs of sparrows gather round the farmyard. Starlings and jackdaws nest in the holes and crevices of farm buildings, ancient and modern. There are still chaffinches, yellowhammers and other finches coming to glean any spilt grain, but not in the quantities they did in the days of the threshing machine. The chaffinch, one of the commonest of British birds, gained its name from being around the farms, whenever corn and chaff were being separated. Today, the collared dove has joined the sparrows in the farmyards. An invader, like the Saxons and the Normans, it has spread, since about 1930, from its homelands in Turkey and the Balkans. It reached southeast England in the early 1950s and is now a common bird round farmsteads and villages throughout Britain. It feeds on spilt grain and is especially common near chicken houses, where grain is fed to the fowls.

The stock dove often nests high up in farm buildings. Its wings, back and rump are blue-grey, with two, short black bars. It lacks the wood pigeon's white shoulder stripe. Unlike wood pigeons or feral pigeons they do not congregate in large numbers. The feral pigeons, are of varied colours and descended from wild rock doves, via generations of domestication for the pot and for racing.

Kestrels and all birds of prey declined in the 1960s, because of the use of organo-chloride insecticides, which are now banned. The residues passed from the vegetation, to the insects and small mammals, to the birds of prey – the end of the food-chain. Kestrels have recovered well. Henry Williamson nick-named them – "Mousing Kee-kee" – from their prey and from their call. Farmers appreciate their control of the rodent population. They nest in holes in the barn walls and take to nest-boxes that some farmers put up for them.

For the barn owl the pendulum has swung the other way. So long the farmer's friend, eating the mice and rats round the grain stores and nesting in his barns, now it is declining to extinction. In the mid 1960s there were an estimated 800 pairs in Devon. By the 1980s there were only about 300 pairs and today there are probably less than 100. The cause may, in part, be due to a global contraction in the range of this widespread species. It may also be linked with changing farming practices. There is less rough grassland and fewer hay meadows and therefore fewer field voles to hunt. The old barns in which they nested have become redundant, demolished or turned into accommodation; so there are less nest sites. Only a handful of pairs remain in the South Hams.

The Barn Owl Trust, from its base near Ashburton, is trying to restore the balance in favour of the barn owl. It runs an education programme for all age-groups, helps install nestboxes at suitable sites and releases and carefully monitors the progress of captive-bred owls returned to the wild. There are many more captive-bred owls kept as 'pets' in Britain than there are wild birds.

The introduced little owl is attracted to farms. Devon farmers call it 'the day owl' as it sits out on gate-posts or chimney tops in broad daylight. Its big, pale yellow eyes appear to fill its small face; it is only about the size of a thrush. They eat beetles and rodents, in about equal amounts. They were introduced into England from about 1880 and reached Devon in about 1920. The South Hams is their stronghold and they have been seen near Modbury, Loddiswell, Aveton Gifford, Bigbury, Salcombe, Prawle, Cornworthy and along the coast.

The plentiful supply of insects, attracted by the piles of dung and the warmth of the cattle, has made farms the traditional site for the swallows to nest. Each spring birds return from South Africa to the same Devon farms where they and their ancestors were reared, building their nests on the rafters of shippens and barns. The farmyard puddles, to provide mud, and the farmyard chicken, whose moulting feathers are used for the silky lining, help make nest-building easy.

Some old farms, with wide, overhanging eaves, have colonies of house martins, that build their mud nests against the wall where it meets the eaves,

Swallows' Nest.

leaving only a small hole. The birds swoop in and out, showing their white rumps and white underparts.

Pied wagtails also feed on the insects. There are few farms without a pair or two, nesting on ledges and crannies in the farm buildings, old or new. They walk round the yard and along the roofs, long tails wagging, pecking at the flies and creepy-crawlies.

In a group of trees near every village, and near many farms, will be a rookery, with between half a dozen to about sixty nests. At any time of the year these garrulous, sociable birds will return to the rookery, apparently to have a chat and to see that all is well back at the old home. In early spring they start bringing sticks to rebuild their nests. There are many arguments. By the end of March they will be sitting on their clutch of about four eggs, swaying in the equinoctial gales. Father feeds both his wife, who does all the sitting, and the young, when they are first born.

The feeding habits of rooks make them both a friend and a nuisance to the farmer, depending on the time of the year and the crops he is growing. Rooks eat earthworms and leatherjackets from the soil. They also eat seeds, including grain before it has sprouted and when it is ripe and flattened by gales. Scaring is often needed when rooks find a freshly seeded maize field. But rooks, like ducks, are curious, comical things. They share with us many human characteristics and chose to live in close proximity to our own settlements; we should show them a mutual respect and tolerance.

Rookeries are often in or by the village churchyard, as at Thurlestone. At the burial of cock robin, in the traditional song, the reply to the question, "Who'll be the parson?" is, "I, said the rook, With my bell and book." The largest South Hams rookery is at Hope Cove, where there were 170 nests in 1999.

The church, with tower or spire, is a landmark in nearly every village. Jackdaws find a way in to the towers to build their twiggy nests. A barn owl used to nest in the tower in the redundant church at South Huish. My first view of the swifts is usually in the first week of May; their wings like black new moons, circling and screaming around a church spire or tower.

In the church roofs, towers and belfries, bats roost and nurse their young. Pipistrelles and long-eared bats are perhaps the most common species. Lesser horseshoe bats are a speciality of the south-west and they may roost in churches as well as in the farms and village houses.

The even rarer, greater horseshoe bats are the ones that hang upside-down, with their wings enveloping them in a cloak. Some are found in old barns and houses but they live mostly in caves. Nigel Mortimer has found Barbastelle bats near Kingsbridge, where they were first found in Britain by George Montagu in about 1803. There are some closely protected bat roosts in the fascinating cave systems, leading from the old quarries of Devonian limestone, at Buckfastleigh. Caves such as Joint Mintnor have a wonderful record of the animals that roamed the South Hams in the Stone Age period, after the last ice age. Where they fell, or were enticed through holes in the cave roof, their bones are piled up below – deer, bears, hyenas. Caves may have been some of the earliest settlement sites for man.

The walls of the churches and the gravestones in the churchyards are beautifully mottled with lichens, thanks to our relatively unpolluted air. Any of our village or town churches will have at least a dozen species – leaves, crusts or tufts of grey, green, yellow and orange, growing from the bare stone. Lichens are a fascinating partnership of alga and fungus; a relationship which was first recognised by Beatrix Potter of Peter Rabbit fame. On the tower of South Milton and Thurlestone churches, Valerie Ransome has found the pink-grey threads of a rare lichen called *Rocella*. On the mortar at Chivelstone church, Barbara Benfield has found a new lichen for Britain, *Thelopsis isiaca*, a Mediterranean species.

The flora of churchyards is always interesting. Good Friday grass, a small, hairy-leaved woodrush, comes out at Eastertime. It seems meet and right that it should flourish in a churchyard. Sweep's brush is another name for it. Lesser celandines are often abundant in the short grass. The well drained parts have bulbous buttercup and hoary plantain. Ladies' smock spreads in the damper corners, where the orange-tip butterflies will be fluttering round its simple mauve blossoms in April. In the redundant church at North Huish, there are beautiful stands of early purple orchids in the wild, but managed graveyard. There were Autumn ladies tresses orchids, creamy, spiralling spikes only a few inches tall, in Buckland-tout-Saints churchyard and I suspect they are present in many of the more coastal graveyards; they just need to be left uncut during their flowering period of late August and early September.

Walls, round the churchyards and elsewhere in the villages, have a special group of plants. Old walls were made with lime mortar and so have lime-loving plants. There is an attractive, wavy-edged fern called rustyback, which only grows on limestone walls or ones made with lime mortar. It is one of a community of small ferns which thrive on walls. Maidenhair spleenwort is the most frequent, with pairs of small leaves down a fine, black stem. Wall-rue has finely divided and twisted fronds. Polypody, which also grows on banks and trees, is rather larger. Walking around any village in the South Hams, you will find these four ferns (*see illustration page 3*).

The mosses which grow on the walls are delightful – shades of gold, green, grey and silver. Through a magnifying glass they are very distinctive and beautiful. Only their names are off-putting. The scientific ones can be difficult to pronounce and the English ones are clumsy; I tend to make up my own! There are four species which are especially common. There is one whose leaves have a golden sheen, *Homalothecium sericium*, or silky wall feather moss. It spreads as a mat, the ends protruding like a peculiar shaped, golden-green, star-fish. When it is dry the ends curl up – a characteristic of this moss. There are three common mosses that form rounded cushions, so they could be called cushion mosses. *Tortula muralis* has long, silver hairs at the tips of the leaves and thin, upright spore capsules on thin, upright stems. *Bryum capillare* has dark hair-points to the leaves and globular spore capsules on nodding stems. The grey cushion moss, *Grimmia pulvinata*, has very long, silver-grey hair-points to the leaves. The spore capsules are buried into the mossy cushion, until they are ripe. Then, the shepherd's crook-shaped stems unbend and raise the spore capsules. From its habit of burying its head, I like to call this grey moss, ostrich moss.

A grey, encrusting lichen, cudbear, or *Ochrolechia parella* grows commonly on walls. Along the top of the walls grey pixie cup lichens, *Cladonia fimbriata* grows like miniature wine glasses. Dog lichens, such as *Peltigera canina*, often grow on walls, where they are more visible than in the banks or grassland, where they also grow. They form overlapping blackish leaves, wrinkled like a Savoy cabbage but only about an inch across. When dry, they turn grey. At the tips spores are produced on chestnut-coloured lobes. The underside of the leaves are white. They are anchored by white threads, which could look a little like a dog's teeth.

Early in the year the top of the walls are green and white with the leaves and tiny flowers of the cress family. Whitlow-grass is the first, followed by hairy bitter-cress and thale cress. Small, bushy plants of thyme-leaved sandwort become common later in the spring and the short red stems and white flowers of fingered saxifrage. Small and pretty grasses, such as fern grass and the silver and small hair-grasses are at home there. Very soon, for lack of moisture, these wall top flowers wither but some are adapted to survive and bloom in the summer.

Ivy-leaved toadflax grows on many walls. The purple flowers develop into small, round fruits. The stems bend to push these fruits into cracks in the wall, so the plant sows its own seeds, earning it the name of 'mother of thousands'.

The most flamboyant flower of our village walls in May, and one that continues to bloom intermittently throughout the year, is red valerian. It creates swathes of bright pink effervescing from the walls. Most of the valerian is bright pink but some is deep red and some pure white. Pellitory of the wall and wall pennywort are other typical species. Some walls have wall pepper, the yellow-flowered stonecrop, as along the wall of the old barracks at Modbury. English stonecrop, which grows on the walls and rocks of Dartmoor and the coast, is also common on village walls, sprinkling them with pink-white stars. The large yellow stonecrop is usually a garden escape. It grows on the churchyard wall at Harford.

Similarly the two bellflowers which flourish on village walls, are introduced; *Campanula portenschlagiana* (which has rather funnel shaped, violet-blue flowers) and *Campanula poscharskyana* (which has more star-shaped, slaty-blue flowers).

Common St.John's wort often occurs along the tops of walls and, where lime mortar has been used, ploughman's spikenard.

Gardens, in village and town, are good nature reserves. In our flower and vegetable patches, attractive annual weeds, such as scarlet pimpernel, join the ones we have planted. Hairy bittercress, red dead-nettle, groundsel and two speedwells, the ivy-leaved and Persian all flower and seed whilst our backs are turned. The ivy-leaved speedwell flowers early and then dies; it is a native. The sprawling, blue-flowered Persian speedwell flowers all through the year and is the most successful weed in our vegetable patch; yet it only arrived in this country in about 1825.

Our lawns can also be interesting botanical experiences. Daisies, dandelions, catsears, yarrow and ribwort plantain grow in harmony with the grass, if not with the gardener. In most of them, the creeping, slender speedwell now grows. From April to June it colours patches of our lawns bright blue and it spreads very rapidly. It was first found in Britain as recently as 1927.

More and more gardeners are reducing the amount of weedkiller and chemical pest control that they use. There is a rich variety of invertebrates. Under the old flower pots and discarded rubbish, granny grigs, the woodlice, hide in their dozens. Your compost heap may shelter the harmless grass-snake or slow-worm. At night, leave your bathroom window open and the light on, and you

Grass Snake.

will be amazed at the number of insects that have flown in by morning. Over a hundred species of moths are common in village gardens, from winter moths in January to hebrew characters in early spring, white ermines in June, silver Ys in August and black rustics in the autumn. Long-nosed elephant hawk moth caterpillars feed on our fuscia bushes. By day the tortoise-shell, peacock, red admiral and painted lady butterflies come to our budleia or ice-plant or michaelmas daisies and their caterpillars feed on our stinging nettles. In spring holly blues often visit gardens. Flies, bees, aphids and ladybirds and many others all provide a rich supply of food for the birds. This is before we have mentioned the caterpillars, the worms and the molluscs.

Villages often have birds at a greater density than the open countryside. The bushes and hedges in the garden, the sheds and the houses make ideal nest sites for a variety of birds. Sparrows and starlings nest in the gutters and downpipes. Any house, new or old, with overhanging eaves, may be suitable for house martins. In 1999 Rod Bone counted 3,000 nests in a survey of the South Hams. Overbecks at Salcombe had the largest colony with 54 pairs. Swallows seem as much at home in the garages and porches of new houses, as in the old farm shippens or church porches. In the Parish of Aveton Gifford, Rod Bone found 100 nesting pairs. Swifts, which nest on beams inside the roof space, use older properties.

Bats will use new houses or old, as long as they are not treated with chemicals that are toxic to them, and they have a rich supply of insects around the villages.

The birds will often choose to build their nests within a few feet of where we humans pass daily. Where wistaria or any creeper grows on a wall the spotted flycatcher may build its nest. This brown-grey little bird, that visits us from Africa, is less common than it was. Old vicarage or farmhouse gardens are traditional sites for them. They perch on a post or branch and make forays to catch insects, usually returning to the same perch.

In a shed or in the garden hedge, robins and wrens nest. Blackbirds, dunnocks, song thrush, chaffinch, greenfinch and even goldfinch will all nest in shrubs and hedges in village gardens and play areas.

In larger gardens, even in the middle of Kingsbridge, Totnes, Dartmouth or Ivybridge, wood pigeons and tawny owls will breed.

In October or November a dark grey-brown bird, with a red tail, may appear in the village. This is a black redstart.It behaves rather like a robin, with an upright stance and is a passage migrant, usually moving on south before the new year.

Our habit of putting out food for the birds has greatly added to the bird life in our gardens. To the nuts come blue tit, great tit and occasional coal tits and marsh tits. In the last few years, long-tailed tits and goldfinches have discovered how to make use of peanut feeders too. Great spotted woodpeckers and nuthatches sometimes come to nuts. Greenfinches are great acrobats on the nut feeder and sparrows and starlings manage less expertly. Especially nearer Dartmoor, the little green and yellow siskins may come to nuts. They seem attracted to the red net bags. On a bird table, or on the ground, seeds and water attract the robin, chaffinches, dunnocks, starlings and house sparrows, with blackbirds and an occasional thrush. Apples and other fruit attract the thrushes. Redwing and even fieldfare will come into our gardens and , in hard weather, they may come in flocks. A few blackcaps spend the winter with us and they will come regularly to bird tables; the males have black caps and the females, ginger-brown.

Big birds such as magpies, rooks and black-headed gulls may take over a bird-table. A screen of wire mesh can solve this problem.

Where there is a healthy population of small birds, there will be predators. Suddenly, across the garden, a sparrow hawk will fly, trying to snatch a sparrow, a blue tit or a starling for his next meal. They are steely-eyed and deadly-taloned but birds of beauty that enrich our village bird life.

Whilst sitting, drawing in his attic studio in Kingsbridge, Mick Loates has seen another bird of prey, circling round St.Edmund's church steeple. It was a peregrine falcon, after one of the jackdaws that nest there. Since then, Mick has seen it several times, returning for another jackdaw dinner.

What did the birds do before electricity? In the last fifty years the pylons, posts and wires have brought electricity to nearly all our homes. Buzzards and kestrels sit on the posts and watch for prey. Yellowhammers, finches, starlings and crows perch on the wires. In spring, the pairs of swallows, hover and perch, side by side on the wires, twittering their love songs. In summer their short-tailed families join them, in a line, wobbling a little uncertainly. Then, in autumn, the migrating swallows may fill the telephone wires, in their hundreds, stacked in double or treble lines, before the long journey to Africa.

Swallows

On the electricity wires in West Alvington, Tim Rhymes saw a pair of bee-eaters in June 1997.

What would our birds of village and town do without electricity wires and poles? Perhaps for every pole taken down, when they become redundant, we should plant a tree.

Since the 1980s, the local council has evolved, with the communities, an environmental Coast and Countryside service. An enthusiastic staff have worked with landowners, parish councils, businesses and wildlife organizations, like Devon Wildlife Trust and Devon Bird Watching and Preservation Society and RSPB. They have encouraged developments that are wildlife-friendly: tree-planting, orchard maintenance, hedge-laying, farm visits, village compost schemes and farm visits for the public. Their programme of walks and events is advertised in special leaflets through the year. Trails along the Avon, Erme, Dart and Kingsbridge and Salcombe valleys have been waymarked. A series of very informative leaflets are for sale on these trails and for the entire coast path. It has produced management plans for special areas, including one for the Area of Outstanding Natural Beauty, that covers much of the South Hams. In involving the whole community in the Agenda 21 proposals for the Twenty-first Century, the Coast and Countryside service helps us respect the past, enjoy the present and plan for the future.

When exploring the South Hams villages and towns, you might choose to link several by a walk, using the lanes and footpaths and perhaps a public service bus, which enables you to look over the hedges. There are trails produced for many of the villages, available at the local shops. Here are some suggestions for grouping the villages:

Ivybridge, Cornwood and Harford.
South Brent, Avonwick, Ugborough and Bittaford.
Buckfastleigh, Rattery and Dartington.
Totnes, Harberton and Ashprington.
Dartmouth, Dittisham and Cornworthy.
Halwell, Diptford, Moreleigh and Woodleigh.
Modbury, Loddiswell and Aveton Gifford.
Ermington, Westlake and Holbeton.
Yealmpton, Newton Ferrers and Noss Mayo.
Kingston, Ringmore and Bigbury.
Kingsbridge, West Alvington and Churchstow.
Charleton, Frogmore and Chillington.
East Allington, Goveton, Ledstone, Sherford and Slapton.
Blackawton, Stoke Fleming and Strete.
Torcross, Beeson, Kellaton and Stokenham.
South Pool, East Portlemouth, Chivelstone and Prawle.
Salcombe and Malborough and Bolberry.
Thurlestone, South Milton, Hope Cove and South Huish.

VI

MARSHES AND LAKES

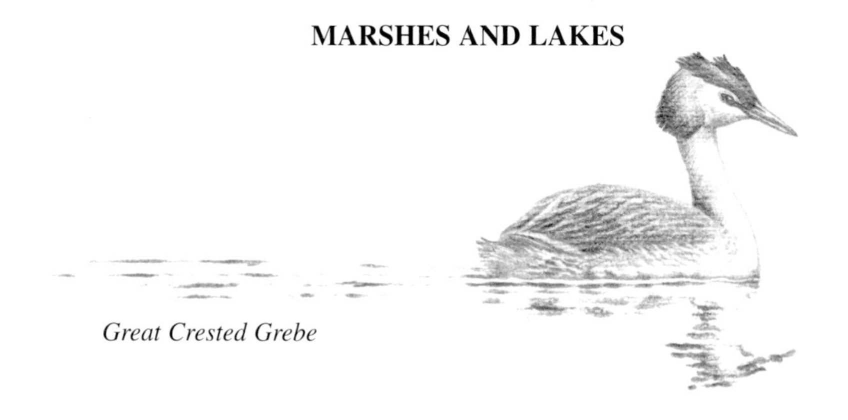

Great Crested Grebe

Lakes are a temporary phenomenon. Once created, they immediately begin to fill with silt. Slapton Ley is the largest fresh water lake in Devon; the largest of a series, formed in the bays between headlands. Slapton, Beesands and Hallsands leys were all formed by a shingle bar, thrown up by the sea along Start Bay, as sea level rose during the last two thousand years. At low tide, after easterly gales have removed the shingle, you can see tree roots and fallen trunks and branches preserved in a platform of clay. They were growing in that clay at about the time Christ was living, before their submergence by sea and shingle.

Since 1961 dedicated birdwatchers and bird ringers have monitored the bird populations of Slapton Ley. These include the late Ray Smith, Peter Ellicott, Alan Searle, Maurice Edmonds, Rod Belringer, Roger Swinfen, Nik Ward, Keith Grant and Dennis Elphick. Dennis Elphick has recently summarised the information in a paper for the Field Studies Council's Journal.

Over 50,000 birds have been ringed during this time, mostly summer migrants. There have been over 350 recoveries, most of which relate to birds retrapped at Slapton. Swans have been recovered on lakes or estuaries from the Tamar to Weymouth. A snipe, ringed in the autumn, was shot in Galway, Ireland, a few months later. Of six kingfisher recoveries, two were in Cornwall and one in Belgium but the remainder were within South Devon.

Five swallows have been recovered in South Africa. Chiffchaff and sedge and reed warblers have been recovered from Senegal and another reed warbler from south west Africa, although most of the recoveries relate to birds migrating through Britain and mainland Europe. There have been about ten recoveries from about 5,000 chiffchaffs ringed between 1961 and 1995, about forty recoveries from about 8,000 sedge warblers and about fifty recoveries from about 10,000 reed warblers. Blackcaps have been recovered in southern Europe and one from Morocco. A willow warbler was recovered: "hit by catapult – still alive" in Ghana. A white wagtail, ringed in the spring, was later found nesting in Iceland. A reed bunting, ringed as a nestling on the Isle of Wight, was caught both at Slapton and by Geoffrey Gush, in east Devon, during the following autumn. Perhaps the most unexpected recapture has been of a red-spotted bluethroat, a rarity from Scandinavia, on its migration to Africa. On average, only about one a year is recorded in Devon, let alone ringed. It was ringed at Slapton on the 21st September 1966. On 14th September 1968 the same bird was caught again, at Slapton!

Slapton Ley – looking over Torcross.

Slapton Ley is the place to look for early and late martins, swallows and swifts. The first sand martins are usually flitting low across the water in early March. Soon after, the swallows arrive; two or three, then dozens and finally hundreds. The white rumped house martins join them, later in April, and before Maytime the early swifts arrive, scything over the surface on thin, black wings. All summer they feed on the myriads of midges, moths, caddis and mayflies that emerge from their larval stage, spent under the water or in the fringe of vegetation;

nowhere in the South Hams can there be a richer source of flying insects. This must be the attraction, on many September evenings, for thousands of migrating swallows and martins to gather high over the Ley. Like interweaving swarms of bees, they arrive and circle; they are so high in the duck-egg, evening sky that some are nearly out of sight. Often, one or more hobbies, most elegant of falcons, will join them, plucking a swallow from among the thousands. It is not until dusk begins to fall that they fly lower and groups peel off to sweep down into the reeds, where they roost for the night – a multitude from all over Britain, perched in lines on the swaying reeds. The car park in Torcross is usually a good viewing station for this demonstration of mass migration in action. The next morning many will continue their way south, leaving the jagged finger of Start Point far behind. Small numbers of swallows and house martins continue hawking over the Ley through October and early November and in some years the occasional bird is seen in December or January, when its fellows are enjoying a second summer in South Africa.

There is also a winter roost of starlings, which begins in late summer and usually builds up to thousands by November; there were up to 100,000 in 1998. Small flocks fly down the valleys, from wherever they have been feeding over the farmland of the South Hams. They join other flocks and wheel around, in ever increasing numbers, settling temporarily on pylons or in trees. The final roosting site is usually in the reeds themselves.

On the water, gulls roost all through the year. All the common species are to be seen, including kittiwakes, and the occasional rarity, such as a ring-billed gull. Winter is the time when many wintering duck arrive at Slapton. Wigeon feed along the margins, when they first arrive from eastern Europe, in September. Many of the grey-billed drakes are still in their eclipse plumage, with beautiful shades of mahogany, ginger and pink. Soon most of them move on to the estuaries, where they spend the winter. Numbers of diving duck build up through the winter; tufted duck, pochard and some goldeneye. A few of the naturalised ruddy duck join them, particularly in hard winters. Red-crested pochard, also originally escaped from captive collections, are seen occasionally. Of the surface feeding duck, mallard are easily the most common but small numbers of gadwall and shoveler are regular. Near the roadside at Torcross birds come close, to be fed – swans, gulls, ducks, including several mallard/domestic duck hybrids of peculiar shapes and colours. Coot and moorhen move jerkily through the water attracted by the hand outs.

There are over a hundred coots on the Ley in the winter. There used to be many more, in pre-war days there were coot shoots at Christmas time, when hundreds would be killed. In the reeds in winter water rails skulk and let out their eerie screams. Up to about ten pairs nest but it is mostly a winter visitor. As summer arrives and the reeds and other water plants start to grow, the reed warblers return from Africa. Their rasping, almost continuous song can be heard

Coot

Coot's Nest

all round the Ley. Mostly they remain hidden in the reed beds, but you glimpse the slender brown bird as it slips through the reeds or flies across from one side of a water channel to another. You may see one collecting the silky fibres from the withered tops of last year's reeds, which they use to line their nests. Those nests are masterpieces of earthquake resistant engineering. The deep cup is woven round several reed stems, a foot or two above the water. The parent sits swaying in a sea of waving reeds, bending gently to every shock, whether the wind comes in gentle puffs or violent gusts. There may be nearly two hundred pairs of reed warblers nesting here each year; their local name is 'Torcross Nightingales'.

The attractive sedge warbler, with its creamy eye-stripe and rust-coloured rump, has become less common than in the past. It prefers the scrub and yellow iris beds along the edge of the leys. There are only about half a dozen pairs breeding at Slapton, in most years, but hundreds pass through as migrants. In contrast the Cetti's (pronounced 'chetti's') warbler is resident. It is a new species for Britain, first arriving at Slapton in the mid 70s and soon increasing in numbers. It too nests more in the scrubby undergrowth at the edge of the reed beds. Dark brown and skulking, it is much the same size as a reed warbler. Its explosive short burst of song is often heard; to see the bird is more difficult. They have built up to a total of over fifty pairs but a very hard winter could reduce their numbers drastically.

Canada geese in Britain are the result of introductions in the eighteenth century onwards. They are now very much at home and flocks of a hundred or more, long black necks craning forwards inquisitively, can be seen around the

Ley and by the little lake nearby at Stokeley Barton. A few pairs nest by the Ley but most disperse to find smaller ponds out on the South Hams farms, where they rule the roost over moorhens and mallard.

Several dozen pairs of coots make their floating nests out at the watery edge of the reed and reedmace beds. It is amazing how well camouflaged the black body is among the reed stems and the white bill looks like just another bleached, broken stem from last year. As soon as the young have hatched from the buff, dark speckled eggs, the parents begin to bring them tit-bits of weed and soon entice them into the water. There may be as many as ten in a brood. At first the fluffy, black babies have striking reddish orange heads but later they become all grey birds, grading into white around the head and on the throat and breast. The Ley's most impressive breeding bird, the great crested grebe, also builds a floating nest. It often nests near the lesser reedmace beds, which show up a brighter green than the common reed beds. From March to May the grebes are at their most demonstrative; male and female side by side, breast to breast in the water, with coppery ear tappets spread and crests raised, as they paddle furiously, creating heart-shaped bow-waves in their love dance.

Great crested grebes did not breed in Devon until a pair or two nested, intermittently, on the Ley in the 1930s and 40s. In 1973 the grebes nested again and this time their numbers rapidly increased. They were to play their part in a fascinating detective story.

The detectives were headed by Professor Kennedy, of Exeter University; his investigation team comprised staff at the university and at Slapton Ley Field Centre. For thirty years they have studied the fish of Slapton Ley and the parasites that live within them. There were, eels, rudd, roach, perch and monstrous pike. They caught a small sample to study the parasites. Many fish they tagged, to study, by recapture, their populations and age group structure. In 1977 they estimated about 950 fully grown pike in the ley; the greatest density ever recorded. But, numerically, the commonest fish in the ley were the red-finned rudd. During the early 1970s there was a dramatic growth in the numbers of the slightly smaller roach. Perhaps, this is what encouraged the grebes and their offspring to stay. The roach and the grebes flourished until the late 70s, when numbers of roach plummeted and rudd regained their ascendancy. The roach began to recover in the early 80s, relative to the rudd, but all the fish declined in total numbers during the first few years of the 80s. Then in early 1985 disaster struck; virtually all the fish disappeared. Who or what had killed them?

Thanks to the monitoring, both of the fish and the water quality, it has been possible to piece together a likely explanation. Firstly, because of nutrient run

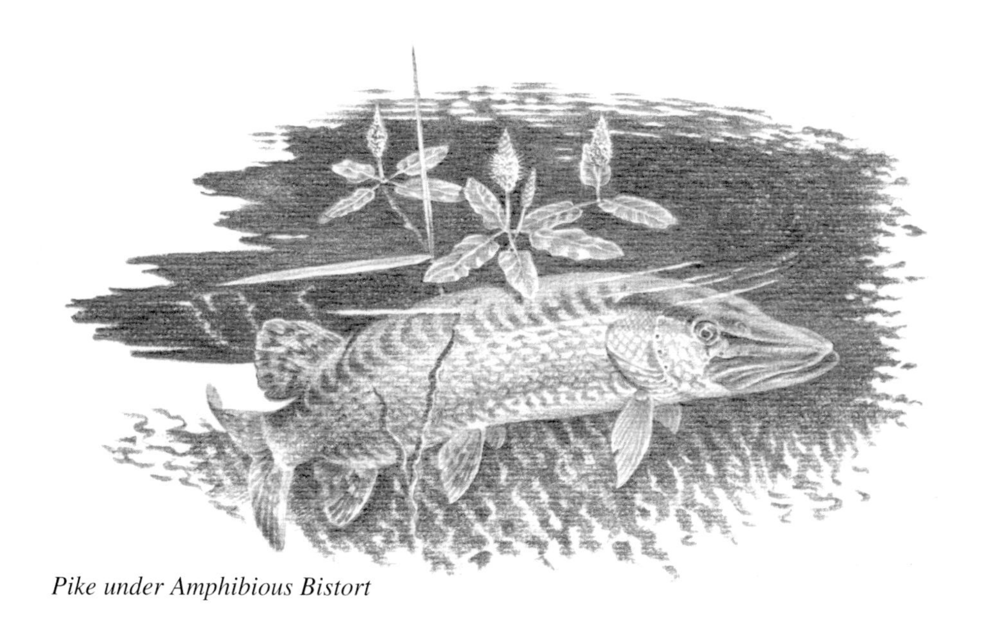

Pike under Amphibious Bistort

off from agricultural fertilizer and excess phosphates from the small Slapton sewerage treatment works, the lake was becoming more eutrophic, in the 1970s. Of all the fish in the Ley, the roach reacted most rapidly to this increase of nutrients. They grew and multiplied faster than any other species. Great crested grebes, arriving in 1973, found a burgeoning population of roach and they and their offspring stayed to enjoy the rich pickings. There were soon about ten pairs on the Ley.

Great crested grebes are the final host of a tape-worm, called *Ligula*. The reproductive segments of the worm are excreted into the water, with the faeces. They are ingested by a tiny, cyclops water flea, which becomes Ligula's first host. In the rich plankton and algal soup, there are millions of water fleas. These, in turn, are eaten by fish, which become *Ligula's* secondary host.

By 1977, thirty per cent of all the roach were hosts to *Ligula*. Roach react particularly badly to this parasite. Infected fish became lethargic – easy prey for the grebes. The grebes ate the fish and were reinfected. *Ligula's* life cycle had come full circle. The long ribbon of segments grew within the gut of the grebe but, as is the case with most successful parasites, without fatal results. For the roach the result was less satisfactory, *Ligula* made them infertile. This is why the numbers of roach plummeted, only to recover after the level of *Ligula* infestation also dropped.

Professor Kennedy proposes a hypothesis that, so long as fish and great crested grebes remain on the Ley, there will be an alternation of rudd and roach dominance, with the roach being the dynamic species, more rapidly increasing and decreasing. He suggests that the decline of all species in the early 80s was due to the build up of ever higher quantities of Nitrogen and Phosphorus producing hyper-eutrophication. The winter of 1984/5 was particularly severe and the Ley was ice-covered for several weeks – the first time in over twenty years. The ice cover further reduced the amount of available oxygen for the fish. It was the coup de grace; they died.

This is the phenomenon known as 'winterkill', which happens commonly in Scandinavia and Canada.

After the crash, Professor Kennedy continued to monitor the fish. Slowly, from a small, surviving population in the higher Ley, they recovered. Rudd at first were commonest but soon roach began to overtake their supremacy, only to decline again a few years later. The grebes had stopped breeding for several years after 1984 but began to increase again, until by the mid 90s there were about ten pairs. The grebes, innocent carriers, of *Ligula*, have returned and Professor Kennedy's hypothesis seems to be confirmed by events.

Local farmers and the water company have worked with the Field Studies Council at Slapton and reduced the run off of fertilizer and other nutrients.

Cormorants' Raft in Ireland Bay.

Although these measures have been taken, the lake is still highly eutrophic. Chris Riley, the reserve officer, who is responsible for the recording and management programmes for the whole Slapton Ley nature reserve, helps monitor the quality of the lake water.

Above: Eyed hawk-moth – "the brilliant eye mark was revealed".

Below: Yellow iris – "stately, winged winged blooms, delicately veined".

The swings in numbers have been less extreme and Slapton Ley has fairly healthy fish and grebe populations, but fluctuations continue. Chris Riley has undertaken an annual monitoring of the submerged waterweeds and these too show worrying fluctuations from year to year.

There are walks leaflets and information at the field centre in Slapton. One can walk the full length of lower and upper leys, on the coastal side. There is a path between the Ley and the main road, which gives good views of the Ley and the reed beds, on one side, and views out to sea, on the other. There is a path along the inner bank of the lower ley, from the bridge to Ireland Bay. In the bay is a raft, anchored to attract resting, wing-drying cormorants. There are hides at the Torcross end of the lower ley, on either side. These give excellent views of most of the waterfowl, including another cormorants' raft. But perhaps the best vantage point for watching the wildlife in general is Slapton bridge, at any time of day or dimpsey.

Anything may pass by, from turquoise flash of a kingfisher, to great, brown bittern. The field centre at Slapton provides guided walks during the summer and a very useful information office.

Recently, otters have increased on Slapton Ley; dawn or dusk at Slapton bridge is a good time to wait quietly, in hope. A few mink hold territories round the Ley; they have been present since about 1970. Studies have shown that they do not inhibit otters. If anything, where they coexist, the otters may cause the mink to move away. Monitoring, in the 1970s, by Chanin and Wise, analysed over 500 mink scats and nearly 2,000 otter spraints – their droppings, left on prominent stones or bridge supports. They found that otters, who feed more in open water, caught mostly fish; about 50% roach or rudd, 25% eels, 10% perch and 10% pike. Ducks formed about 5% of their prey, with just a few small mammals. Mink feed more round the edge of the leys and their diet is only a third fish, a third birds, especially coots and moorhens, and a third small mammals.

Over the water, during the summer months, Daubenton's bats hunt during the hours of darkness. Feeding on the insects flying above the surface, just as the swallows and martins do during the day.

There is a vast hoard of invertebrates, especially insects, that prey on each other and feed the birds and other larger animals. Many species of small and often unusual flies and beetles live round the Ley. Spiders' webs are strategically placed to sample them. One species, *Tetragnatha*, specialises in waterside habitats and nightly builds a web to catch the smaller flying insects. In the early morning you brush through the webs that span across the footpaths and they are speckled with the dozens of insects that have met a sticky death. This spider has a tubular shaped, creamy body and holds its long, front legs extended forwards. The most conspicuous insects are the damsel and dragonflies. Along the edge of the Ley, in summer, are blue and blue tailed damselflies. Sometimes you see a mating pair, joined in a copulation wheel, their abdomens curled round to each others' thoraxes to deposit and collect the male's sperm. They can fly together in this position. Red damselflies are less common. In mid-summer the larger dragonflies, such as the steely blue, black-tailed skimmers, patrol along their patch of waterside. There are many moths, including the eyed hawk-moth. This hawk-moth lays its eggs on pussy-willow and, in the higher ley, islands of pussy willow are rapidly replacing the reed beds as the dominant vegetation. Once, when we were looking for reed warbler nests, we saw an eyed hawk-moth, nearly two inches long, settled like a dead, crumpled leaf, at the base of a reed stem. I gently moved one of its upper wings (*photo page 75*) and the brilliant pink and blue eye mark beneath was revealed – enough to scare away any hungry, insect-eating bird.

A pair of blue-tailed damselflies joined in a copulation wheel.

The vegetation of British lakes proceeds, by a number of stages of succession, from open water to oak woodland. In the lower ley there are pondweeds, growing from the bottom of the lake, amphibious bistort, with floating leaves and short, pink spires of flower and white water lilies. Towards Torcross the overlapping green leaves of the water lilies, create an island of shining green, from which the globular white stars of the flower heads emerge. Apart from providing resting places for the dragonflies, the leaves are also the favoured food for the larvae of the pretty, white and brown, china-mark moth. As the larva grows bigger, it not only feeds on the lily leaves, it also cuts small segments to construct a protective case, rather like a caddis fly larva's. Reed is the dominant vegetation round the edges of the Ley, with some of the smaller reed-grass and patches of reed-mace, (mostly the thin maces of the lesser but also some of the fatter greater reed-mace) and branched bur-reed. In the spring there are colourful patches of the golden marsh marigold. Soon after follow the pale blue of water forgetmenot and the tall sword-leaved tufts of the yellow iris, with its stately, winged blooms, so delicately veined. In the summer the bright purple spikes of purple loosetrife show among the reeds and the deep blue of skullcap. Water mint is a common plant, often growing out into the water. The pink spikes of marsh woundwort are common and, usually by standing water, the nettle-like leaves of gipsywort, with its small, white whorls of flower. In some sheltered ponds of open water, water mint is joined by the pink flowered bog-bean. Water dock often grows by the edge of such ponds. Where wooden walkways cross the wetlands, between Ireland Bay and the Slapton sewage works, there are miniature forests, two feet high, of water horsetail; a family of plants that dominated the vegetation of the coal age forests, with giant trees a hundred feet high.

The Ley at Beesands, correctly called Widdicombe Ley, has a similar fauna and flora. It is a Slapton Ley in miniature and it is in some ways even more appealing. There are less crowds and there is no main road with traffic roaring past. Beesands has a good pub – the Cricket Inn – and a fresh fish stall. Local bird watcher, Perry Sanders, spends much time at Widdicombe Ley, making it his special patch. Most of the birds one sees at Slapton Ley can be seen here and often the views are closer. It is the best place to see that elegant grey-brown duck, with a black bottom, the gadwall. Both the surface feeding duck and the diving ones are here, the autumn and spring birds of passage, a few breeding pairs in summer and the full variety in winter. Recently, during a cold snap in the winter there were up to five smew and a goosander, joining the pochard, tufted, mallard, shoveler, wigeon and teal. The Mike Rogers hide provides shelter and wonderful views of the birds throughout the year. Nothing is too far away. There is good wheelchair access from the car park. The hide is named after the local farmer, who has done so much to encourage cirl buntings and all wildlife on his farm. Please respect the privacy of his land adjacent to the hide. It was built by the Devon Bird Watching and Preservation Society in 1995 and opened by Hilary Soper. There are useful charts of the most frequently seen birds and dragonflies and a notebook in which all are invited to put their sightings.

Further along the coast at Hallsands, there was, once, another small ley but it is now silted up and covered by old osier beds, spreading willow scrub and reeds. Marsh marigolds brighten the edge and the Cetti's warbler announces his presence with an explosive burst of song. One winter a bittern visited the old osier beds.

Unless man or the ravages of the sea interrupt the natural succession, in a few hundred years time Slapton and Widdicombe Leys will look like the one at Hallsands.

Just as the sea has worn away the soft Meadfoot Slates to form Start Bay on the east, on the west it has worn them away, forming Bigbury Bay. Here too streams have been blocked by bars; in this case sand rather than shingle. In less than a mile, immediately south of Thurlestone, there are three parallel streams, which reach the sea. Once they would have had open water lagoons but now only South Milton Ley, resembles the Start Bay leys. From the north they are: Thurlestone Marsh, South Milton Ley and South Huish Marsh. Thurlestone and South Huish have been reclaimed and provide grazing for cattle but there are still ditches and patches of reed. Always, in the winter, they have been liable to flooding, when several hundred wigeon and teal have dabbled in the shallow flood water. Wintering snipe are attracted to the wet grassland. Ruff have been frequent passage migrants, sometimes staying most of the winter. Flocks of Canada geese have become common, sometimes with an exotic escapee, such as a barnacle goose. A whiskered tern visited Thurlestone Marsh.

South Milton Ley still has a little open water and has a fine, continuous reed bed. The way to the sea, is blocked by a transient sand bar. Regularly, in

South Milton Ley.

times of flood, the stream breaks through the bar, rushing in spate, down the beach to the sea, creating South Milton's answer to the Grand Canyon. Henry Williamson, described this, the reed beds, the sand dunes and the rocky coast in his 1930s novel, *The Innocent Moon*, which is partly set around South Milton and Hope Cove.

South Milton Ley is now one of the Devon Bird Watching and Preservation Society's nature reserves. This is thanks to thirty years' devotion by Bob Burridge, the voluntary warden, who has worked with the land owners and farmers to secure this fine wetland. He first discussed the idea of a reserve with Miss Ilbert, owner of much of the reed bed. Through her he was able to trace the wildlife story back into the last century, by studying the number of wildfowl shot in the estate records.

Bob has ringed the birds rather than shot them. With Vic Tucker, Harry Huggins and many others, he has ringed thousands of birds during the last twenty years. There has been lots of excitement. One autumn he performed a delicate rugby tackle to catch a merlin falcon, sheltering in the reeds and found it had been ringed as a fledgling on the moors of Wales, that summer. Recently, on a hunch, he played a recording of the call of the rare penduline tit, which has been extending its range, and soon afterwards the first Devon record of a penduline tit flew into the strategically placed mist net. Bearded tits have spent the winter in the reed bed and one year a pair nested here. Most years he sees a marsh harrier, quartering low over the reed bed on its long, finger-spread wings. Reed and sedge warblers, not only breed but use the marsh as a feeding station on passage. Bob's long-term studies have shown that there is a regular movement of these warblers between Slapton and South Milton. In winter snipe abound, shooting skywards in broad zig-zags and giving their squelching boot calls. At the upper end of the marsh, where the public footpath crosses by the sewage works, there is an information board with a beautiful artist's impression of the reserve, by Mike Langman. Here is a good place to stand on a frosty winter's morning and wait to see the slate-blue water rails stalking along the sides of the ditches, probing with their curved beaks.

Reed Warbler's Nest.

Thanks to negotiations involving South Hams District Council, the Environment Agency and 'Devon Birds' Society', South West Water have ensured that the outflow from the sewage works will not add unwanted nutrients. After the normal processing stages, there is a special filter bed, planted with reeds, to mop up most of the residue.

Thanks to Mr. Darke, the farmer, South Huish is also now a nature reserve, as well as a grazing area for his cattle. Scrapes have been dug and banks constructed, so there is some open water throughout the year. There is a good viewpoint from the refreshment kiosk. Another excellent painting by Mike Langman shows the birds you might see: the dabbling duck, often including some shoveler, and groups of lapwing and oystercatcher, which come in from the shoreline at high tide.

It is always worth scanning the posts and wires of the fences, by any of these marshes. Wheatears are especially common birds of passage in spring and autumn. Whinchats and the resident stonechats also use these frequently for perches. There may be small flocks of linnets and goldfinches. In October and November there is usually at least one black redstart, flicking his rufous tail.

Great Crested Grebe on its nest.

In addition to these more extensive marshes, there are small but very important areas of marsh and lakes and ponds tucked away on farms all over the South Hams. The marsh at West Charleton is another gem and is described in the chapter on estuaries.

At Salcombe, the Coast and Countryside Service has dredged out a pond at Hangar Marsh, behind the car park at North Sands. A hide will give views of the pond. The increase in dragonflies and other insects should attract more migrating swallows and martins and the occassional hobby. Perhaps a pair of great crested grebes will come over from Slapton to nest here!

VII

THE ESTUARIES

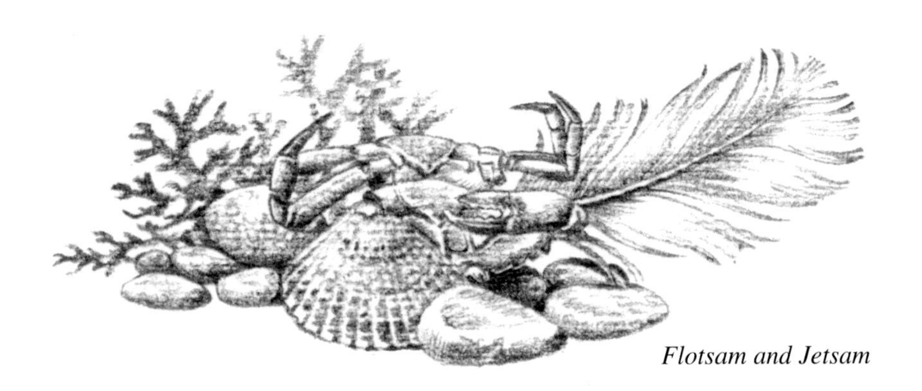

Flotsam and Jetsam

The Yealm, the Erme, the Avon and the Dart are the four true estuaries of the South Hams. Kingsbridge Estuary and its continuation in Salcombe Harbour is a ria, having no river flowing into it, only minor streams.

All five 'estuaries' share a salt water habitat, diluted to varying extents by the fresh water streams. All are tidal, having two tides a day, about twelve hours apart. (*Maps showing the true estuaries are on pages 21–24.*)

Along some of the fringes there is saltmarsh. In the firmer mud there are colonising forests of glasswort – like succulent cactus trees, a few inches high – with some seablite. There are patches of the invasive *Spartina* grass, except on the Kingsbridge estuary. Sea plantain, sea arrow-grass, sea spurrey and sea milkwort are common in most of the lower saltmarshes, growing in swards of saltmarsh grass, *Puccinellia.* In spring the early and common scurvy grasses are in flower. The taller, mauve-flowered, sea aster is prominent later in the year. There are patches of the bushy, grey sea purslane and, in the drier saltmarshes, some thrift. Tufts of saltmarsh sedge, with its long bracts overtopping the seed heads, are frequent, sometimes at the edge of the bare mud. On the higher marshes, saltmarsh rush becomes more common. At the edge, above high tide mark is a band of a tall, greyish grass, sea couch, with some spear-leaved orache and sea-beet, the ancestor of our spinach and beetroot.

Where fresh water seeps down to the estuary, there are patches of sea club-rush, common reed or, occasionally, the grey-blue stems of grey bulrush. The

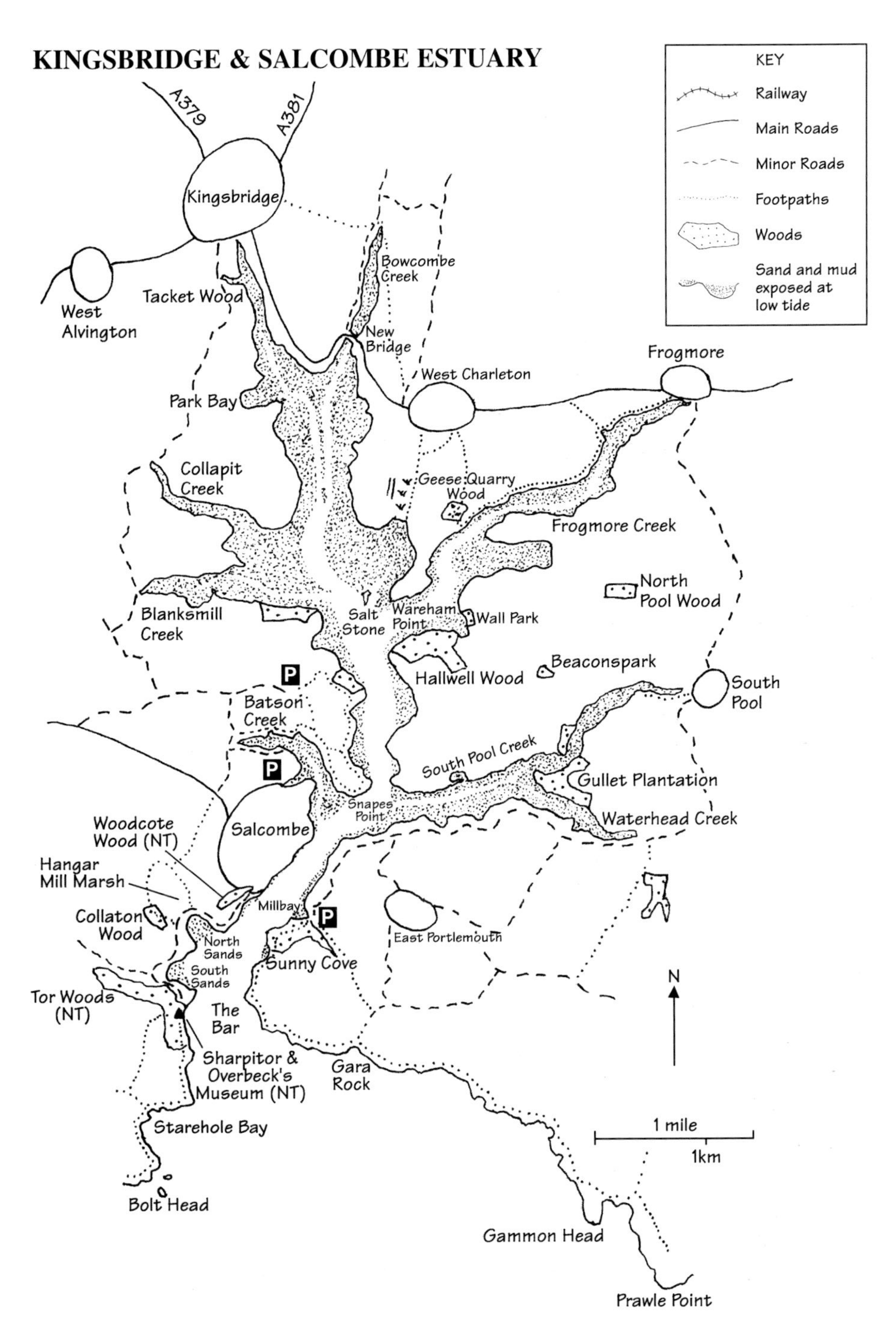
KINGSBRIDGE & SALCOMBE ESTUARY
KEY
Railway
Main Roads
Minor Roads
Footpaths
Woods
Sand and mud exposed at low tide
A379
A381
Kingsbridge
West Alvington
Tacket Wood
Bowcombe Creek
New Bridge
West Charleton
Frogmore
Park Bay
Collapit Creek
Geese Quarry Wood
Frogmore Creek
North Pool Wood
Blanksmill Creek
Salt Stone
Wareham Point
Wall Park
Hallwell Wood
Beaconspark
South Pool
Batson Creek
South Pool Creek
Gullet Plantation
Snapes Point
Waterhead Creek
Salcombe
Woodcote Wood (NT)
Hangar Mill Marsh
Millbay
Collaton Wood
North Sands
South Sands
Sunny Cove
East Portlemouth
Tor Woods (NT)
The Bar
Sharpitor & Overbeck's Museum (NT)
Gara Rock
N
Starehole Bay
1 mile
1km
Bolt Head
Gammon Head
Prawle Point

more extensive, grassy saltmarshes, are roosting and feeding sites for curlew and wigeon. The curlew peck and probe for invertebrates. The wigeon graze the saltmarsh grasses.

Seaweeds clothe the rocky edges below high water mark. Where only the spring tides reach, is a narrow, fragmented zone of channelled wrack – a short branched and tufted plant with grooved stems. Below that is a wider zone of a slightly larger weed, flat wrack (sometimes called spiral wrack, from its twisted appearance). This blends in to the widest zone of knotted wrack, which is larger again. With the knotted wrack, at its lower end, may be some bladder wrack. The bladder wrack has pairs of bladders, which pop. The knotted wrack has no mid-rib and its bladders are single, spreading the whole width of the long, flexible fronds. Where the rocky fringe descends low enough, there is a further zone of saw wrack.

On these seaweeds live grey, sea firs; apparently plants but really colonies of small animals, related to jellyfish. On the knotted wrack, a dark red tufted weed grows, *Polysiphonia.* Rough winkles and flat winkles browse on the seaweed and are well camouflaged in yellows and browns. Rough winkles that live in estuaries are quite smooth shelled, only on exposed shores do they develop the typically ribbed shell. Hundreds of side-shrimps shelter beneath the wet fronds until the tide returns.

These animals provide food for the small flocks of turnstones that visit the lower parts of the estuaries, flicking over the weeds, to reveal the creatures beneath.

The autumn and winter are the best times for bird watching on the estuaries. In April and May there may be whimbrel and a few other migrants passing through but from late March until mid-July is a quiet time on the estuaries. The broods of young mallard, shelduck and swans compensate for the lack of waders and other wildfowl. Just a few non-breeding oystercatchers remain. From mid-July curlew begin to arrive and soon after the redshanks are back. The autumn brings common sandpipers and many unexpected passage migrants, little stint, curlew sandpiper, ruff, perhaps even a rarity such as a pectoral sandpiper.

On every estuary the gulls are probably the most numerous of birds. Herring gulls are with us throughout the year but it is the black-headed gulls which are the most common. In June and July they return from their nesting colonies in Dorset or Hampshire, in their hundreds and feed on estuary and ploughlands through the winter, until they leave again in March. Some common gulls spend the winter with us, they have green legs and are slightly bigger than black-headed gulls. A few great black-backed gulls frequent the estuaries and,

Black-headed gull.

particularly in the early spring, the yellow-legged lesser black-backed gulls. When there are gales, huge numbers of these black-backs may shelter on the estuaries.

At low tide the mud-flats are the feeding grounds for wading birds and shelduck. In the mud, there is a greater density of invertebrate life than in any other habitat. There are worms, such as ragworms and lugworms, with the silvery cat-worms, near the sea, where the substrate becomes sandier. There are small burrowing crustacea, like *Corophium*, beloved of redshanks. The minute spire shells, *Hydrobia*, in their millions, feed the shelduck, which push their shovel beaks through the soft surface mud, to sieve out the snails. Deeper in the mud are the bigger shellfish; the peppery furrow shells are very common, with carpet shells, sand gapers and cockles. Wherever you see oystercatchers busy probing with their thick, orange beaks, they have most likely found cockles. The curlew, with their long beaks, can reach down to the U-shaped burrows of lugworms and the deep sand gapers but, with the sensitive tip of the bills, they can also pick *Hydrobia* or small worms from the surface.

Where the green gut-weed, *Enteromorpha*, and, more sparsely, small eel-grasses, *Zostera*, grow over the mud-flats, there is poorer feeding for waders but flocks of wigeon graze there.

In the surface pools and the channels, which continue flowing through the mud-flats at low tide, greenshank, the queen of the waders, wade, dart and snap up oppossum shrimps and fish-fry.

They are much scarcer than the orange-legged redshanks; they show up paler and slightly bigger than the redshanks and when you get really close you can see the grey-green legs and slightly up-tilted bill.

The beautiful little egrets, with fine plumes from head and back, feed in a similar way. They are even more active, high-stepping along the water's edge, showing yellow feet below slender black legs. They snap up the shrimps and fingerling fish, with black, needle-like bill. Their numbers have built up from about half a dozen, in 1989, until now there are over a hundred, between the five estuaries. Each July and August there is a fresh invasion from Brittany. The birds stay the winter but many return south in the spring, leaving only a few behind. They are already nesting along the south coast of Britain. In which of our five estuaries will they choose to nest? On the continent they often nest in the same trees as the herons, although a month or two later. They are an exhilarating addition to our estuary birds.

There are now often more egrets than herons on the estuaries. Each estuary has one or two small heronries, from about half a dozen to a dozen pairs. The herons are more patient in their feeding habits, waiting stock still for long periods and suddenly lunging forward to catch an eel or a flounder.

As the tide comes in, flounders move up over the mud banks and mullet follow the tide up the creeks. Shrimps and prawns spread in and opossum shrimps, gather where salt and fresh water meet. All our estuaries have long stretches where oak woods reach down to the water's edge. On the overhanging branches, or on the gunwale of a boat, a kingfisher waits for small fish to pass and then plunges. Each estuary has at least one pair of kingfishers. Larger, black fishermen, the cormorants, come up with the tide, taking their share of the mullet and flounders. Some diving duck, goldeneye and red-breasted mergansers winter, particularly on the Kingsbridge estuary. There, one or two great northern divers, come feeding on crustaceans and fish. I have seen one surface with a crab in its beak. Divers may be seen near the mouths of the other estuaries.

Occasionally, an Atlantic grey seal will fish in the estuaries, following the rising tide. Sometimes, one may take up nearly permanent residence. One at Salcombe has taken to sunbathing on a floating box, reserved for keeping live crabs and barely raises her head when you pass by in a boat.

The most spectacular fisherman is the osprey. George Montagu recorded them in the autumn on the Avon, in the early years of the nineteenth century. After a period when persecution drove them to extinction, as a breeding bird in Britain, they are breeding widely in Scotland again. Each autumn at least one visits our estuaries, to take a few mullet, before it continues its migration to the rivers of central Africa.

The Yealm Estuary is almost entirely a muddy estuary. It is fed by three main streams, at its northern head. The most westerly flows into Cofflete Creek. Cofflete Creek is narrow and sheltered,running south for just over a mile before it meets the main branch of the estuary at Steer Point. You can walk to the head of the creek, along the public footpath from Spriddlestone, and look down its length, or go to Steer Point and look up. In rough weather, the wintering flock of

Atlantic Grey Seal in Salcombe Harbour.

up to a hundred shelduck, may shelter in Cofflete.

Silveridge 'Lake', is the middle stream, crossing the main A379, between Yealmpton and Brixton, and flowing through the grounds of Kitley House. Below Kitley it has been dammed to form Kitley Pond. This has a good population of mallard and up to about thirty teal in the winter. Coots and a few dabchicks are there, with diving duck – pochard and tufted.

Below the dam, the water tumbles over the stones to rush into a muddy basin. The channel that winds its way through the mud is appropriately named Mudbank Lake. This basin is virtually separated from the main estuary by the causeway, at Warren Point, that took the track of the old railway, across the creek. It is now long disused. In the channel float the little, bob-tailed dabchicks, mallard and teal. By the channel, heron, redshank and greenshank stand, wade or run; it is clearly rich in life.

The River Yealm itself enters the estuary from the west. Below Puslinch, there is a saltmarsh delta at the head of the estuary, where curlew and wigeon often gather and occasionally Canada geese. Sunk in the mud beyond are the stumps and branches of old trees, like tusks and limbs of prehistoric mammoths. For a mile the creek widens, until at Broad Ooze, the creek is over half a mile wide. Here most of the gulls, wigeon, shelduck, curlew and redshanks will be feeding. It is possible to follow the track of the old railway, along the north bank of the main creek, as far as Warren Point if you obtain permission from Kitley Estate. The main channel is close to the north bank for much of the way and greenshank, herons and egrets may be quite close. At Warren Point you can look, from the old causeway, into the Kitley basin.

A good viewing position for most of the estuary, is near Steer Point. From the road you can see across Cofflete Creek. On the other side there is a path, which goes from nearly opposite the brickworks, to the eastern foreshore, which it follows for several hundred yards. There are views upstream towards Warren Point; at high tide there may be about two hundred wigeon bucking up and down on the choppy water. The planted, evergreen oaks, which fringe much of the northern shore, flicker silver and green, in a strong wind. Downstream you can see down past the quay at Thorn, to the moored yachts, towards Newton Ferrers. From Noss Mayo, you can walk along Newton Creek, that separates Newton from Noss Mayo. It enters the estuary from the east and is nearly a mile long. It is too narrow and too busy to support much wildlife, but redshanks and oystercatchers, probe in the mud and mallard and muscovy ducks dabble and have illicit love affairs by the slipways. The road on the southern side leads past Ferry Wood, from where I once saw a red-throated diver in mid-channel, to the coastal path. Walking westwards to Mouthstone Point, there is a dramatic view of the open sea and the island of the Mewstone in Wembury Bay. Herring gulls cry and wheel about the cliff-tops and down below, in the turquoise sea, shags dive for pollack and mackerel.

The Erme is a simple but very attractive estuary, fed by the River Erme, south of Ermington. It is tidal for about three miles, downstream from the weir below Sequer's Bridge on the A379. For the last mile it becomes sandy. The land on either side of the estuary is owned by the Flete Estate and access is only by permission. So the Erme is largely undisturbed and, for its size, has more wildfowl than you might expect. For over fifteen years Harry and June Huggins have been making monthly counts of the wildfowl and waders of the estuary.

Canada geese graze on the marshy meadows either side of the upper part of the estuary, where the river remains very narrow. A green sandpiper may be flushed from the edge of the river here. The first access point is along the lane that leaves Holbeton and runs east to the estuary. This is where the estuary first begins to grow wider. There is a glimpse of the river, the salt marsh, with sea club-rush and *Spartina* grass and perhaps a distant view of mallard, wigeon or teal but there is no access to the estuary side here. There is a private drive along to Efford House, which is opened for charity events once or twice a year. Please respect the privacy of this drive. However there is a public bridleway from Holbeton across the fields to the estuary bank by Efford House. Again there is no right of way upstream or downstream but you can scan in both directions with your binoculars. Nowhere is the estuary wider than about two hundred yards, so great distances are not involved. In the summer, there is a fine spread of naturalised, pencilled cranesbill, by the track. In winter there may be over a hundred wigeon in view and sometimes as many teal. There are not more than about twenty shelduck. Flocks of curlew and lapwing may rest on the saltmarshes. *Spartina* grass has taken a major role in establishing the extensive saltmarshes on the Erme. About forty curlew winter on the Erme and about twenty redshank, scattered over the mud and beside the channels. In the main channel you may see a few dabchicks.

Wigeon.

At Pamphlete Pool, now silted and overshadowed by trees, Elaine Hurrell sat for hours, in the 1960s, listening for the whistling of otters. The otters are back on all the estuaries, but very seldom seen.

The last mile of the estuary is best approached from either Mothecombe on the west or Wonwell on the east. Leaving your transport, where the road widens, near Wonwell beach, you can walk back up the road, or take the parallel route by the public footpath, through Wrinkle and Furzedown Woods to Blackpost Cross. From the crossroads, there is pedestrian access, down a narrow lane, sloping steeply through Tor Wood to the river. The woods themselves are private but the lane comes out on the foreshore, by a house with a wonderful position. It overlooks the only side creek of the estuary, which is about four hundred yards long, ending below Clyng Mill and Oldaport. To the right is a grassy saltmarsh, fringed with sea purslane, grey-green and bushy. It gives a good vantage point to stand and look at the waders and wildfowl, egrets and herons. You can see over the little creek and upstream towards Efford House. The estuary is so sheltered from the south-westerly winds that the oaks can be still dappled with orange and green in late November. Flocks of wigeon gather in the little creek.

The drakes' chestnut heads with yellow blazes, powder-puff pink breasts, grey and white bodies and pointed black tails look beautiful against the shining, slate-grey mud.

Here I have seen two male egrets competing for the favours of a female. One chased off his rival, walked up to the female and with grunts and growls they danced, half jumping, half flying over one another's heads, black legs and yellow feet dangling in mid-air. After a few minutes they flew off down the creek, under the arch of the stone bridge and out of sight.

At low tide you can scramble along the narrow, seaweed-covered foreshore below Tor Wood and walk southwards along the sands back to Wonwell, completing a triangular walk of about two and a half miles. Between Tor Wood and Skerril Coppice the river narrows but soon widens again, as the main channel swings across to the far side of the river. A spit of sand has built up and is covered by couch grass, sea radish, some sea sandwort and, unexpectedly, scattered reeds. Looking south over the sands and silver ribbon of water, there are sometimes up to a thousand gulls – black-headed, herring and black-backed – and a few oystercatchers. The sand is scoured with swirling holes and runnels by the fierce and dangerous current that rushes in and out. Beyond, the sea surf thunders on the bar at Erme Mouth.

Half a mile above Aveton Gifford bridge there is a weir, which marks the upper limit of the tides in the Avon estuary. For the next four miles the Avon meanders gently to the sea. It is the most sandy of any of the estuaries; the last two miles having broad shoals of water-rippled sand.

Rod Bone has walked the banks of the estuary, since he was a child, over fifty years ago. He knows more about the wildlife of the Avon than anyone. For forty years he has completed the monthly counts of wildfowl and he still has a spring in his step. Above the old bridge at Aveton Gifford, grazed, freshmarsh grassland stretches out to either side of the river, across the wide flood plain. In winter it is liable to frequent flooding. Dark tussocks of soft rush spear through the grass, where many snipe probe in the soft ground. At high tide, flocks of wigeon, teal, curlew and lapwing settle by the floodwater. A few green sandpipers always winter here, along the narrow runnels through the marsh. For several winters, through the 1980s, family parties of Bewick's swans, between five and eight birds, stayed grazing on the marshes, before returning to their Siberian breeding territories in the spring. Rod found a killdeer – a very rare plover, wind-blown from America – feeding by the flood-water, in February 1999. Mute swans and Canada geese are there, throughout the year.

In spring black-tailed godwits have stayed on the marshes for a week or two, raising hopes that they might, one day, nest. Flocks of whimbrel, 'the seven whistlers' as they are called locally, stop to feed at first light, on their journeys north to Scotland or Iceland. Where a few fields have restricted grazing, there are meadows of yellow iris, rushes and ragged robin, and here sedge warblers and reed buntings nest during the summer. Bats, from their roosts in the farmhouse roofs, flicker above the marshes to catch the moths and other abundant insect life.

Inside the embankments that prevent the river flooding, on all but the highest tides, there is a strip of grey bulrush swamp and saltmarsh. On this a pair of swans may attempt to nest. Rod Bone has recorded every swan nesting on the estuary and how many young have been raised; he has constructed rafts under the nests, so that they are not flooded by the spring tides.

For a short time, in the 1980s, a lagoon to the north of the bridge, opposite the Avon Bridge Garage, was flooded daily by the tides. The wading birds it attracted, especially during the autumn migration, were remarkable. There were flocks of dunlin, curlew sandpiper, ruff, ringed plover, as well as lapwing, redshank and greenshank.

Downstream of the bridge, on the south side, beyond South Efford House, is another freshmarsh area, with drainage ditches. This is also used by the wildfowl and waders, particularly at high tide. Moorhen and wintering water rail creep through the club-rush along the ditches. Greenshank scythe their bills through the water, where bullocks have made a clear way down to the ditches. One winter a lesser yellowlegs, from America, spent several months on South Efford Marsh. There is a substantial sea-wall around the marsh, and a path along it. Scrub has grown up and stonechats perch on the twig tops and on the fence below the bank. In the autumn, whinchats, with their pale eye-stripes, also perch on the fence posts and wire. It was while walking along this sea-wall with Rod Bone, that we saw a wryneck, perched on a fence post, looking at us, with his neck tilted to one side, accentuated by the snakey lines in its buff and grey plumage. During the war, the sea-wall was breached and Rod remembers the huge flocks of wigeon and teal that came to the marsh then, until the breach was repaired in the 1950s.

The freshmarshes of the Avon have great potential as a wetland nature reserve. Above the bridge, the lanes either side of the river give excellent views of the marsh. The round trip, along the lanes, past Knap Mill, to Hatch Bridge and back, through Hatch and Venn, is about four miles and makes a delightful walk. There is also a spur path from Hatch Bridge, across the marshes towards Hatch.

From the car park, off the roundabout by the Fishermen's Rest pub, at Aveton Gifford, you can walk or drive along the tidal road towards Milburn Orchard, except at high tide. The car provides a very effective, mobile hide but an oblivious birdwatcher, stopped in the middle of the road, can be frustrating and rather dangerous to other motorists. There are attractive patches of varied saltmarsh by the roadside. Oystercatchers, redshank, greenshank and gulls feed and roost upon the mud. In the channel, swans swim sedately and, in the winter, dabchicks dive in the shallow water. Egrets patter there, to disturb oppossum shrimps from the soft mud, and herons wait patiently for the next meal to swim by.

At high tide, when there is little disturbance, cormorants fish in the deeper water and perch on the black and white stakes, that mark the line of the road. Many vehicles have tried to play 'Israelites and Egyptians' with the rising tide and almost suffered the fate of the Egyptians in the Red Sea.

There is an interesting diversion to follow the footpath by the side creek before Milburn Orchard. The path goes up the east side and you can turn right along the lane and paths, to return to Aveton Gifford, via Waterhead, or turn left and immediately left again to walk down the west side of the creek, to Milburn Orchard.

Stakes Road – tidal – with Spartina growing in the mud.

I love to spend time in the saltmarshes along this little creek. Near the parking space, by the roadside at Milburn Orchard, are patches of bright green, sea club-rush. Taking groups of children gives me the excuse to imagine each type of saltmarsh inhabited by alien creatures. Sea club-rush, *Scirpus maritimus*, I imagine inhabited by the Scirpans. If you look carefully among the club-rush, during July and August, you will see creatures leaping. When they rest for a moment you see a long greenish animal. It could almost be a giant grasshopper. It has very long feelers, eyes on stalks and, from its rear-end, a long knife-like protruberance. This is an ovipositor, for laying eggs, and the animal is a short-winged conehead – a type of bush-cricket. But for me it will always be a Scirpan!

The little crabs, that crawl over the mud, through the mini-forest of glasswort, are Salicornians. Any life in the cord-grass, is classed as Spartinan. On the bushy, sea purslane grows a small, feathery red weed, *Bostrychia scorpioides* – another name to conjure with. Do the natives of the sea purslane world avoid it?

If you continue on along the foreshore beyond Milburn Orchard, for over half a mile, you walk by the best saltmarshes that I know. On the firm mud, north from Doctor's Wood, glasswort stretches for several hundred yards; nowhere have I seen such a forest. *Spartina* – cord-grass – originally caught the silt and accelerated the rise in level of the main saltmarsh. It is divided by sinuous creeks, edged with sea purslane. The *Spartina* is now beginning to die back and saltmarsh grass, sea aster and the other saltmarsh plants are increasing instead.

The curlew and wigeon gather out on this saltmarsh and on the similar marsh on the other side of the river. Groups of egrets often stand in artistically placed groups, waiting for the tide to go down, so that they can continue fishing. They also perch in the trees at Stadbury or Doctor's Wood. Perhaps Rod Bone will be able to encourage them as he does the swans.

As the tide goes down, gulls and the wading birds come down to the mud to feed. In autumn, from Milburn Orchard, with the redshanks, you may see ringed plover and dunlin and sometimes curlew sandpiper and little stints. Once Rod phoned me to say a pectoral sandpiper was there. The mud is a little sandier and seems to attract passage migrants.

Downstream the estuary bed is progressively sandier. There are more oystercatchers and more gulls, including the black-backs. These last, seaward reaches of the estuary are best approached from Bantham. There is a public footpath, giving views over the sands, which leads upstream to the head of Stiddicombe Creek. Here, as almost anywhere on the Avon, you may glimpse a kingfisher. The path goes by Stiddicombe Wood and, from just before you enter the wood, you can see the herons feeding their ugly, grey offspring in their tree-top nests. Please do not disturb them.

From Bantham you can usually see most of the flock of up to sixty swans, which feed in the estuary. Sometimes they are upstream, sometimes down beyond the thatched boathouse. The Avon is easily the best estuary for swans, having a rich food supply of weed and invertebrates suitable for them. On the gravelly shoal between Bantham and Cockleridge, there are always birds of interest. Oystercatchers are commonest here, with good views of lesser and great black-backed gulls, heron and egrets.

Across on the sand spit at Cockleridge, sea holly and sea sandwort grow just above the tide-line. In August the prickly, grey sea holly has lovely blue globes of flower, surrounded by buzzing bumble bees. Amongst the marram and finer grasses on the rest of the spit, autumn ladies tresses orchids are present, in late summer.

The walk round Bantham Ham is one of our favourites. We have been there on Christmas Day, with a biting east wind and in high summer, with crowds of people, but we are never disappointed. Evans Estates are to be thanked for preventing Bantham becoming a mass of icecream parlours, slot machines and obtrusive caravan sites. It provides pleasure for thousands of us and yet it remains rich in wildlife.

Marram grass is the plant that is primely responsible for holding the dunes of sand blown in from the beach. It tops the dunes and slowly other plants fill in between the clumps. These include the creeping stems, kidney leaves and pink and white striped trumpets of sea bindweed, the sand sedge, sending up sprouting leaves in straight rows, and the bright golden-green moss, *Tortula ruraliformis*. Two poisonous plants are pioneer species in the sandy hollows; the common bittersweet, or woody nightshade, and the rare henbane.

Small dune snails are very common on the dunes and their shells, together with the bones of rabbits, which are also common at Bantham Ham, are blown into 'graveyard' corners. Most are rounded snail shells; one of several similar species was first described by Montagu. The white, spire-shaped shells, with gingery markings, are *Cochlicella acuta*, a species that often rests hanging onto the stems or leaves of plants.

The calcium in the snail shells, blown sea shell fragments and rabbit bones produces a sandy soil suitable for plants which normally grow on chalk or limestone. The yellow-flowered ladies' bedstraw and the pink pyramids of pyramidal orchids are specialities of the grasslands at Bantham. In some places the wild clematis, traveller's joy or old man's beard, a typical chalkland plant, sprawls over the sand dunes.

The succession which leads to a grassland sward brings colourful flowers, like birdsfoot trefoil, greater knapweed and even ragwort, all of which attract insects. There is a thriving colony of the white and black marbled white butterfly. The caterpillars of the six-spot burnet moth feed on the birdsfoot trefoil, as do the common blue butterfly larvae. The burnet moths fly by day and are very conspicuous, with their warning red and black colour scheme, on sunny, mid-summer days

Marram Grass.

By one of the paths, narrow-leaved everlasting pea, a pinky-purple flowered relative of the sweet pea, climbs up the bramble scrub. It is only common in the southwest.

In the scrubby bushes that are scattered over the Ham, linnets and stonechats nest. The twittering of linnets follow you on a summer evening, when you walk on the Ham. From the low cliff-top you can look out to the surfers' paradise, where the long rollers come sweeping in past Burgh Island. Gulls and a few sandwich terns dip over the waves. Along the water's edge a few white, sanderling may run in and out at the sea's edge.

In holes in the cliffs below, sand martins nested for at least a hundred years. They were recorded in the 1880s. About ten pairs were still nesting through the

1970s and early 80s. I took a school party to look at them and I remember the boys being more interested in a topless sunbather, nearby! In 1986 two pairs of sand martins may have bred and that was the last record. Just perhaps, if we can be dissuaded from climbing down the cliffs, the martins will return, if and when their numbers begin to increase internationally.

The River Dart is the longest of our five estuaries. The tidal stretch is about eleven miles, from Dartmouth to Totnes. The weir above Totnes marks the upper limit of tides. There is an attractive walk by the riverside, from Totnes to the weir. Wood anemones and marsh marigolds grow beneath the alders and pussy willows. Up in the branches parties of green and yellow siskins may be feeding on the alder cones.

Burnet Moth Caterpillars and Pupa.

Salmon and sea trout work their way upstream in the autumn. The heron and the otter both take their share.

Where the little River Hems joins the Dart, by Snipe Island and the sewage works, tufted duck dive to the bottom for seeds, molluscs and crustaceans.

Through the town, while picnicking on Vire Island or on the quays, the mallard and black-headed gulls arrive en masse, to accept your crumbs. There has been a feral Egyptian goose joining them for several years.

On the east side of the river is a quay, from which pleasure steamers ply up and down to Dartmouth. This is an indication of the size of the Dart; it is a considerable river. The trip down to Dartmouth takes over an hour. A path continues for nearly half a mile to Long Marsh, a pleasant picnicing area and managed as a nature reserve, with attractive wetland plants, scrub, planted trees and clearings and ponds, which attract many butterflies and dragonflies. A beautifully executed interpretive picture by Beverley Curl and sculpted panel, by Nic Meech, describe the variety of species.

On the other side of the river a path continues beyond Totnes to Sharpham Marsh. This is a splendid area for wildlife. The marsh is partially enclosed by an old sea wall. On a very stag- headed oak tree, growing along the wall, cormorants often perch. From the disused sewage works you can make a short diversion from the footpath to walk a little way along the wall and back through the reeds, experiencing the unique atmosphere of life in a reed-bed – a world of its own. Reed beds are the most extensive habitat, with reed and sedge warblers nesting in the summer.

There are also patches of sea club-rush and, by the runnels that wind into the marsh from the wide breach in the old wall, wide fringes of saltmarsh grass and sea aster. Little egrets fish along these runnels. Tony Soper has flushed green sandpipers from here. Reed buntings often nest in the club-rush and stay through the winter, feeding in the reed beds or in neighbouring fields.

In winter there are water rails squealing in the reeds and many snipe hidden away in the marsh. Curlew gather on the saltmarsh grass and small flocks of wigeon. The public footpath runs just inland of the marsh, by Linhay Plantation and through a new, mixed planting of trees. You can see the birds down on the marsh without disturbing them. The path turns off the farm track and climbs steeply to Lower Gribble Plantation; from here is a fine view over Sharpham Marsh and up Home Reach towards Totnes. You can see across the river to the grassy saltings, where black-headed gulls gather on Fleet Mill Reach. The path continues into Ashprington.

From Ashprington there is another path which leads eastwards, down a spur to Ashprington Point, opposite Stoke Gabriel. To the left, you can see the river snaking upstream, and to the right, Bow Creek. From Ashprington Point you can see redshank, oystercatcher and curlew, feeding on the mud and, at high tide, the oystercatchers and curlew feed and roost on the grassy slope. Tony Soper has often seen more than a dozen cormorants perched on the end of Ashprington Point at high water, drying their wings and digesting their wrigglesome food.

Bow Creek is one of the most attractive, rewarding parts of the estuary. At the head, between Bow and Tuckenhay, there are pleasant hostelries, one of which has a beautiful and realistic painting of the wildlife of the estuary, mounted in its car park. The painting even shows the blurred wings of a kingfisher, flashing past, by the overhanging branches of the oak trees. Clouds of white doves, rise above the roof-tops, from their dove cotes by the pub and comical processions of mallard, and duck of mixed parentage, beg from the quayside customers. There is a good footpath which follows the southern bank of Bow Creek for about a mile. From there you have a grandstand view of heron and egret fishing and of shelduck floating on the water or padding across the mud. In June there is usually at least one flotilla of sheld-ducklings. Redshanks and a few greenshanks, roost on fallen branches or rocky spits along the northern shore, at high tide and pace the water's edge as the tide recedes and floods. Oystercatchers and curlew probe in the mud-flats.

The path itself winds under trees for part of the way. There are some bushes of butcher's broom as well as ferns, woodland flowers and pink purslane. Under the tall, golden beeches there are flocks of chaffinches, pecking at the beech-mast, in autumn. And I always check them to see if there are some white-rumped brambling with them. In the thickets you may see that other white-rumped finch, the bullfinch – a glimpse of bright pink breast and the single, weak piping contact call of his mate.

Before the path turns inland to Cornworthy, there is an open view down towards the mouth of the creek. Wigeon may feed in the channel here, at low tide, or drift up on the flood. Along the foreshore the ribs of a rotted boat rest forlorn.

Between Cornworthy and East Cornworthy, there is a magnificent view, from the roadside, of almost the whole estuary. Beyond Totnes, in the north, Dartmoor rises with the double tors of Haytor on the horizon. To the south, you can see to the boatyards at Noss, near Kingswear.

If you travel on to Dittisham and leave your transport, you can walk, at low tide, round Lower and Higher Gurrow Points and up to the head of Dittisham Mill Creek, at Brambletorre Mill. There is a car park by the foreshore, on the east side of Dittisham. From here you can walk down to the piers and quays of Lower Dittisham, where there is a passenger ferry to cross to Greenway Quay. Greenway House was the home of Humphrey Gilbert, the Elizabethan explorer. Between the quay and the well-placed youth hostel at Maypool, herons have nested for many years, especially in the old Scots pines. The herons move somewhat from year to year and there are other sites, further upstream.

Walking northwards, along the foreshore, you have a view across to the gravelly shoal of Flat Owers. This is particularly good for wading birds and gulls. Suddenly, you feel a more marine influence, for herring gulls far outnumber the black-headed gulls, that have been constant companions from Totnes downwards. Now there are also great black-backed gulls, pirates of the sea. Along either foreshore, turnstones may be flicking over the seaweeds. On the mud-flat between Lower and Higher Gurrow Paint, Tony Soper has regularly seen ringed plover, especially in August and September. The plovers have a distinctive way of running a few steps and then pausing; the clear black ring round the white neck is another easy diagnostic mark. Joining the redshanks, oystercatchers and curlew, parties of dunlin run over the mud and along the water's edge. From Higher Gurrow Point, you can see Sandridge, the site of the house where John Davis, another Elizabethan explorer, was born. A few herons may nest in the trees nearby.

In Dittisham Mill Creek, a pair or two of shelduck stay to breed in the summer. Along the upper part of the creek is a public footpath, with much easier walking and a narrow fringe of saltmarsh, with sea aster, spiking through the water at high tide.

Tony Soper has discovered that Old Mill Creek, two miles downstream from Dittisham, is the best place to see common and Arctic terns. They fish by diving headfirst into the water, to snatch sandeels and other small fish. They pass in spring and particularly in late summer and early autumn, on their way south, to winter off Africa or, for the Arctic tern, off the pack-ice of Antarctica.

Sea Aster and Jersey Tiger moth.

On the mooring and marker buoys in the busy waterway between Dartmouth and Kingswear, gulls and cormorants perch. It is worth checking for Sandwich terns, for they also perch on buoys. These are our commonest terns, coming through at the same time as the so-called common terns but continuing sometimes into October. The Sandwich tern has a black, not red bill, with a yellow tip. The black cap is not so sleek, being ragged at the back but its tail is forked, like all the terns, earning them the appropriate name of sea-swallows.

In the boat park in Dartmouth town and along the quays there are usually mute swans. Opposite the boat park, ferries leave for Kingswear and the trip up to Totnes. But my favourite boat trip is the ferry down to Dartmouth Castle; it is very good value. You have a splendid panorama of Dartmouth and Kingswear and watch the water below you growing clearer and choppier as you near the sea. Herring gulls, wheel around their nesting cliffs, Sandwich terns dive for sand eels and call raspingly, like a creaking gate, and the slim, 'green cormorants' – the shags – swim underwater for pollack and mackerel. Dartmouth Castle itself is perched on the cliffs, at the mouth of the estuary, built with stone brought from the Kingsbridge Estuary, in barges, over five hundred years ago.

Tony Soper has written a detailed account of the 'Wildlife of the Dart Estuary', full of historical detail and giving a sailor's perspective. He sails up from the sea to Totnes, reaching parts that we landlubbers cannot reach.

In 1992, I wrote a book about 'The Wildlife of the Salcombe and Kingsbridge Estuary', when it was declared a local nature reserve. Now it is republished, with some changes and new photos. For details of what to see where, I recommend it to you. The book has many references to George Montagu, who came to live at Kingsbridge, with his mistress Eliza Dorville and her son Henry, in 1798. He

Portrait of George Montagu by kind permission of the Linnean Society

studied the estuary and was the first to describe nearly a hundred new species, from sponges and sea slugs to the bottle-nosed dolphin, the roseate tern and the rock pipit. Many anecdotes are included in the book on the Salcombe and Kingsbridge Estuary.

The importance of Montagu remains central to any account of the estuary but there have been many new developments in the years since the book was first published, in 1992.

Plumose Anemones growing by 'Egremont' in the Kingsbridge and Salcombe Estuary.

The Harbour Office now has a conservation officer, who is working with fishermen, farmers, local businesses, yachtsmen, naturalists and tourists to keep the estuary thriving both economically and as a local nature reserve. Montagu would approve of the way Nigel Mortimer, the conservation officer, always refers to the diatoms. They are the microscopic algae, which tinge the surface of the mud khaki, and are the first link in most of the food chains which support all life on the estuary. Montagu, a pioneer in microscope work, first studied their beautiful silica skeletons two hundred years ago.

There are now useful interpretation boards at Whitestrand, in Salcombe, at Bowcombe and at Charleton Marsh. The carved board at Bowcombe viewing platform, by Nic Meech, is a practical diagram of how the food chain works and, at the same time, a sculpture of quality. Similarly the board before Charleton Marsh always gives me pleasure. I gave a pencil scribble to Trudy Turrell, at the South Hams District Council, to suggest some of the highlights of a year on Charleton Marsh and Beverley Curl has transformed the scribble into her own evocative work of art. An acknowledgement to these artists should be given.

At Charleton Marsh, Wal Towler and the Rogers family have worked with the wildfowlers and the Council to enhance this wildlife gem, with extra scrapes, some new planting and a grazing-free refuge. We can help by keeping to the footpath side of the marsh. Across at Coypool, the British Trust for Conservation Volunteers and Hilary and Tony Soper have been restoring some of the old duck decoy pond.

Sandwich Terns

The South Hams Society has restored one of the estuary's lime kilns, at Frogmore, through the skill of master mason, Michael Sutton. They have also financed the partial restoration of Fort Charles, at Salcombe.

There is now an on-going mapping of the sea-grass beds at Salcombe and the salt-marsh communities throughout the estuary, co-ordinated by Nigel Mortimer. Margaret and Peter Quick have co-ordinated an effort to monitor the swan population, building rafts under the nests, recording dates of egg-laying and hatching and sending any birds found dead for an autopsy. Swans on the estuary have been ringed since the 1960s but it is now proposed to colour ring all the swans, to trace their movements within and outside the estuary. Please report the registrations of any colour ringed birds you see to Margaret Quick.

The estuary has an extraordinarily rich fauna of invertebrates – sponges, sea-squirts, worms, crustaceans – of fish and of birds. The numbers of birds involved are so much greater than any other South Hams estuary. In mid-winter there may be over 5,000 birds using the estuary and it only measures just over four miles from the Quay at Kingsbridge to the Harbour Bar.

Heron.

In summer, the estuary looks a picture but there are few birds. Some herring gulls, a few cormorants and non-breeding oystercatchers remain. The herons bring their grey young to fish by the creeks. The swans have their cygnets, the shelduck their bobbing flotillas of ducklings and the few kingfishers are nesting in holes, stinking of fish. By July the curlew are returning, soon followed by redshank, greenshank and Sandwich terns. An influx of egrets join the small summering group, which may have nested, after the herons, in the tall, waterside trees. In September the osprey is most likely to visit. In winter the numbers of wildfowl build up until, by January there may be a thousand wigeon, a thousand dunlin, a thousand black-headed gulls and, if there are gales, a thousand other gulls, mostly great black-backs, sheltering from the weather. Between two and three hundred shelduck, teal, curlew, oystercatchers and redshank also spend the winter here, with about a hundred grey plover and brent geese.

In that part of Frogmore Creek I call 'diving-duck bay', there may be a dozen or more goldeneye and red-breasted mergansers. Grebes too favour this bay. As many as ten great crested and little grebes, or dabchicks, gather here and near the Saltstone, diving so frequently they seem to spend more time under the water than on it. Black-necked and Slavonian grebes are also regular but scarce visitors to the estuary and, in the winter of 1999, Peter Cummings watched a red-necked grebe diving by the fish quay at Salcombe.

When the wildfowl and waders take to the air, weaving patterns against the winter skies and filling the air with their calls and the sound of their wings, Kingsbridge Estuary is a place of magic.

There are several good paths from which you can explore the estuary. You can walk along the road from Kingsbridge to New Bridge and then follow the lane up Bowcombe creek and return over the hill, by a footpath, to Kingsbridge. Another footpath goes from the end of Frogmore creek and you can follow the foreshore out to Wareham Point and return up Charleton Marsh, to Charleton village. At low-tide only, you may walk along the foreshore from the end of Blanksmill Creek to Rowden Point, but the tide comes in swiftly. There is access to the saltmarsh at the very head of South Pool Creek. The best overall views of the estuary are from the National Trust land at Snapes Point and over to Batson, where you may also hear the cirl buntings singing. From Salcombe or East Portlemouth you can follow the coastal path to the Harbour Bar and beyond. A sea eagle was shot near Sharp Tor in 1909; Montagu kept two, in an aviary, were they from a local nest, perhaps above Starehole Bay?

APPROXIMATE MAXIMUM NUMBERS OF BIRDS ON SOUTH HAMS ESTUARIES

	Yealm	Erme	Avon	Kingsbridge	Dart
Great-crested Grebe				15	1
Mute Swan	20	10	60	15	30
Brent Goose				100	
Shelduck	100	20	30	250	50
Wigeon	300	200	300	1500	100
Teal	50	200	60	250	50
Mallard	150	150	70	200	150
Tufted Duck	20			20	120
Pochard	50	5		5	5
Goldeneye	5		5	40	
Red-b Merganser			5	30	
Canada Goose	50	20	20	50	20
Oystercatcher	25	30	50	300	25
Lapwing	50	70	100	80	50
Ringed Plover		5	30	30	
Grey Plover			10	100	
Snipe	10	10	20	20	20
Turnstone	10		15	10	10
Curlew	150	100	70	350	80
Whimbrel	5	5	20	20	5
Bar-tailed Godwit			5	20	
Common Sandpiper	5	5	5	5	5
Redshank	70	20	50	250	80
Greenshank	5	5	15	30	5
Dunlin	30	10	50	1000	20

VIII

THE COAST

Cirl Bunting

The estuaries bring us to the coast, the sea-laced hem of the South Hams. Nearly every visitor will walk at least part of the coastal path. The attraction is not only the sea, there are the rock formations, the colourful succession of plants, the wealth of insects and the bird life. The coast path provides a narrow ribbon from which all these appear, unwinding against the constantly changing seascape.

From the bare rock, lichens are the first plants to grow. Grey species, like sea ivory and cudbear, grow highest up the cliffs, a little lower *Xanthoria* and *Caloplacca* species form a band of yellow and orange and nearest the sea is a band of black lichen, mostly *Verrucaria*, splashed by the waves at high tide. Within this general pattern are many other common and rare species. Slapton Field Centre has a course on our local lichens every year. From the detritus of crumbling rock and old lichens, enough nutrients and anchorage are provided for the first flowering plants to take root.

On the cliffs themselves rock samphire is common and, where the cliff is crumbling, rock sea lavender. Where there are shaded overhangs two ferns may spring from crevices in the rock; sea spleenwort and the south-western rarity, lanceolate spleenwort.

In spring the lilac flowers of early scurvy grass and in summer the pale pink stars of English stonecrop are sprinkled over the almost bare rock like salt. Other plants common on these thinnest soils are buckshorn and sea plantains, sea spurrey, sea storksbill, wild thyme and sheepsbit – a scented rainbow, which takes the breath away.

Above: English Stonecrop growing from schist rock.

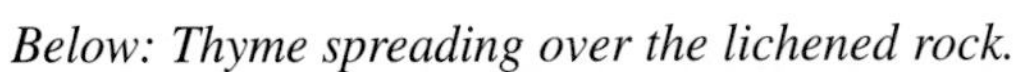

Below: Thyme spreading over the lichened rock.

But, for me, the flowers that conjure up the typical scene of our beautiful coast are, thrift, sea campion and kidney vetch. In May, thousands of thrift's pink pompoms of flower rise from the matted green cushions, clumps of white sea campion speckle the grassy cliffs like nesting seagulls and mixed with them are the yellow heads of kidney vetch set in their soft green foliage. Another name for kidney vetch is lady's fingers, for the leaves are divided and resemble pale green, velvet gloves, soft enough for a lady's hand. The small blue butterfly lays its eggs in the seed heads of kidney vetch but it has not yet been found in the South Hams. The equally rare thrift clearwing moth, whose larvae feed on the leaves of thrift, does occur.

In the thin soils above the rocky cliffs, you sometimes find the unobtrusive dwarf chickweed. This small, waxy, blue-leaved chickweed has white flowers that only open in bright sunshine. The little hair-grasses are common, both the small and silver species, and a close relation of the abundant annual meadow-grass, *Poa infirma*. It is paler and weaker than the annual meadow-grass. Only in the last decade have botanists realised that *Poa infirma*, early meadow-grass, is common along the South Devon coast, on these thin rocky soils.

On the flat cliff tops, the flora often resembles heathland. Bell heather and ling are frequent species and sheep's sorrel gives a red flush to the ground. There is heath speedwell, milkwort, early forgetmenot, mouse-ear hawkweed, trailing St.John's wort and saw-wort, which also grows in the heathy clearings of Andrew's Wood.

By the path, where it passes through rocks, Portland spurge grows. As the summer progresses its green leaves turn red. On bare ground by the path may be birdsfoot – its flowers pale and very small but its seedpods long and curved like a bird's claws.

In the short grass, common dog violets are very common in the spring and sporadically they bloom again in the autumn. The small pearl-bordered and dark green fritillary butterflies, that often flutter away from you down the coast path, both lay their eggs on violet leaves. Where the grass is cropped very short, spring squill puts up its pale blue stars and curved leaves in spring and, in autumn, its rarer cousin, the autumn squill replaces it with mauve spikes.

In the grass are hundreds of insects, including long, brown click beetles, whose larvae, wireworms, feed on the roots of the grasses. Lay them on their backs on your hand and they leap into the air with a click, like some Christmas cracker toy. There are a rich variety of grasses along the cliff paths. Red fescue, which has fine, wiry leaves, is perhaps most common. There is a variety which has bluish leaves. A very big grass, with wide, shiny leaves is probably tall fescue, also known as reed fescue.

Small Pearl-bordered Fritillary Butterfly.

On the grassy slopes, the white umbels of wild carrot follow after the thrift. In some places there are dapplings of magenta from the finest of the cranesbills, bloody cranesbill.

The clover family is prolific. By the paths there are haresfoot clover, hop trefoil, common yellow trefoil, birdsfoot trefoil, on which the caterpillars of common blue butterflies and six-spot burnet moths feed, and the hairy and long-fruited birdsfoot trefoils. As well as the common spear and creeping thistles, the slender, or seaside, thistle is frequent and, on some slopes, the deep pink-purple nodding heads of the musk thistle, are very common. Occasionally, by the path and in sandy places carline thistle grows. The metallic, dull gold flower heads look almost like dried flowers.

Prickly ox-tongue, with yellow flowers and prickly leaves that feel just like the rasp of a bullock or cow's tongue, is a common plant in the longer grass and it goes on flowering all through the summer and autumn.

Where there is deeper soil, bracken spreads in extensive patches. Under it primroses and, especially, bluebells thrive, nurtured by the dense shade after their flowering. A cliff-slope washed with bluebells and dappled with thrift is a glimpse of heaven.

The small umbellifer, pignut, wood-sage and wood spurge all occur where the bracken towers above in the late summer. The larvae of the small sooty-black moth, the chimneysweeper, feed on pignut and the moths fly by day, so can be seen flying round the white flowers.

Because the coastal path is worn bare by the tread of so many feet, it is easy to see a cross-section of the invertebrates that live among the coastal vegetation. Butterflies rest on it, perhaps attracted by the heat absorbed by the bare earth or rock. The well-camouflaged grayling butterfly closes its wings and swivels itself in a direct line with the sun, so that its shadow is only a thin line and it is virtually invisible. Many caterpillars are squashed, by our feet – 'clumping two boots'.

Oak eggar and drinker moth caterpillars are particularly common but we have seen hawk-moth, tiger-moth, white ermine and countless unidentified caterpillars. Grasshoppers, especially the field grasshopper, pause on the edge of the path and we have seen both dark and great green bush-crickets. These last are about four inches long and bright green, like locusts. They are restricted to southernmost England. The females have a long sword-like ovipositor which Bryan Ashby has seen being pushed into the path vertically, to lay the eggs in the thin soil.

Both ants and mining bees are common by the path, their presence betrayed by big mounds, often thyme-topped, or tiny mounds of soil around small holes. Watch these holes for long enough and you will see a bee alight and scramble down the hole. The late Malcolm Spooner and his wife Mollie, spent many hours identifying species of mining bees, and botanising, along this coast path.

Where streams cross the cliff path and make their way down to the beach, is a completely different kind of flora. Reeds often grow here, and water-cress and fools' water-cress, water mint and the tall, pink and white willow-herb, codlins and cream. Fleabane is common and attracts many butterflies. Bittersweet and silverweed spread at ground level. As the streams trickle down, over the rocks to the sea, brookweed, a small white-flowered plant, characteristically grows. These wet rocks, often at the top of the old rocky, wave cut benches, are also typical habitats for tall docks, maritime varieties of the curled dock and sometimes the rare shore dock.

Patches of scrub, growing along the coast are important for insects and birds. Wild madder, a big, clambering shiny green relative of goosegrass often grows up into the lower parts of scrubby bushes. The wrinkled, black larvae of bloody-nose beetles feed on their leathery leaves, The rounded, adult beetles can often be found walking slowly and suicidally across the footpath. In early spring you may see another black beetle, the oil beetle, walking on or by the path. They are elongated, with short wing cases that leave most of the long, segmented abdomen uncovered.

The bushes are mostly blackthorn or gorse, with occasional elder and hawthorn and scrub elm. On the thorn bushes, you may find white webs. They are not the work of spiders but of masses of brown caterpillars, which have clear blue lines down their bodies. They use the webs as shelters or sun-loungers. When they have pupated they will hatch into lackey moths.

On the gorse bushes, both the common and shorter, western gorse, the red, leafless stems of dodder grow parasitically, eventually producing pink globules of blossom. In May and June, green hairstreak butterflies are often seen fluttering around gorse. When they settle they close their wings and the undersides are leaf green, with a hair's width streak of white. A gorse shield bug is associated with this prickly bush and another shield bug is common on the bramble thickets at blackberry-time. In the bushes, stonechats, whitethroats, linnets, yellowhammers and our special rarity, the cirl bunting, may all build their nests.

The stonechats are very distinctive, sitting on top of a bush or bracken stalk, flicking their tail and making a sharp sound like two stones chinking together.

George Montagu, who first found the cirl bunting by the Kingsbridge Estuary in 1800, was also the first to describe the nesting habits of the Dartford warbler. After a run of mild winters, the Dartford warbler is spreading back into the South Hams and may continue to nest.

Kittiwakes at Hallsands – all in pairs at their nests.

Wheatears are very common at migration times, sitting upright in the short, cliff-top grass, and flying off, showing their white arses. A late migrant is the black redstart, most often seen between October and December – a dark grey bird with a red-rusty tail.

The gull on the cliffs is the herring gull; everywhere it is common. Until this century great black-backed gulls were uncommon but now there are many. Some lesser black-backs – slate-grey backs and yellow legs – spend the winter with us but many more move northwards, from Europe and North Africa, and pass through in February and March.

Kittiwakes may be seen offshore, from March till the autumn, especially off Bolt Head, near where they used to nest. Now they only nest regularly at Hallsands, where there is a colony of several hundred pairs. The fulmars, gliding on straight wings, return from the Atlantic earlier, before Christmas, and a few pairs nest along the whole extent of our coast, from Plymouth to Torbay.

Floating on the water like penguins, you may see a few brown and white guillemots or black and white razorbills. They occasionally fish offshore in the South Hams but do not nest; their nearest colony is at Berry Head, near Brixham. Out to sea you may see these auks flying past in greater numbers.

Cormorants nest on offshore islands, like the Mew Stones and Burgh Island. Shags are much more common, the sea ravens they are sometimes called. They are smaller than cormorants, their necks are more sinuous, their plumage has a more oily, green sheen and in spring they sport a curling, black crest. I savour Henry Williamson's name for a shag – 'Oiligrin'. Oiligrin nests on shaded ledges along the cliffs and in steep gullies.

The raven itself is a bird of the cliffs, as well as a bird of Dartmoor and woodland. They build their nests on the cliff face, using gorse twigs and a lining of sheep's wool. You can tell him from his crow cousins by the huge size, his wedge-shaped tail and the sonorous "Kronk" of his call.

Oiligrin the Shag

Flocks of jackdaws gather near their nesting holes in the cliffs but the choughs, which bred in Montagu's day are now never seen.

Birds of prey are a frequent sight. The kestrel is most common, feeding mostly on mice and voles and hovering, motionless on her 'wimpling wings', even in a blustery wind. Williamson named her, 'Mousing Kee-kee' and 'Chack-check' was his name for the peregrine. Peregrines once more nest round our cliffs, feeding on jackdaws, feral pigeons and other birds. After the catastrophic decline in the 1960s and 70s they have recovered. Buzzards perch on the rocky eminences and have become catholic in their tastes, as well as rabbits, they will take voles, moles and adders, which one commonly sees basking near the path on a sunny spring morning.

THE SOUTH HAMS COASTLINE

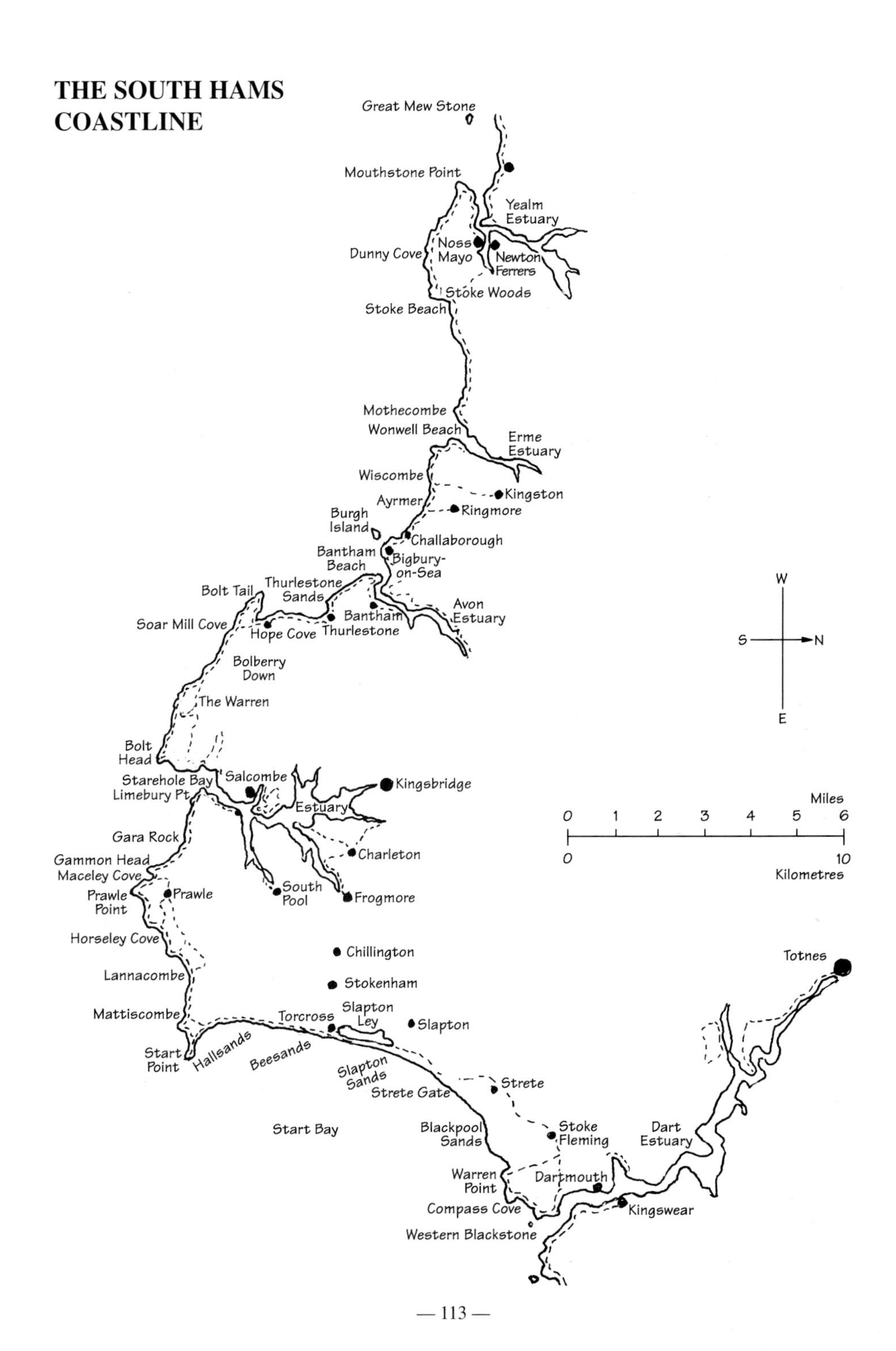

Rabbits are the most obvious mammals along the coast, cropping the grass and providing food for buzzard and fox. Foxes and badgers dig out their homes in the deeper soil, often under the scrub of blackthorn and elder.

Walking the coastal path is a tiring but uplifting experience whatever the weather and whatever the time of year. Most stretches have more ups and downs than you experience during a walk on Dartmoor. The walk from the mouth of the River Yealm to Stoke is an exception. You can park near the coast at about a mile either side of Netton farm, on the lane that runs parallel to the coast, or make a round trip from Noss Mayo. Depending on the route you take, the walk is between about five and seven miles. From Mouthstone Point you look west to the angular slab of the Great Mew Stone, where the Navy fires shells overhead and the cormorants make their nests, safe from disturbance. There is a good path, with no steep climbs, which follows an old carriage drive and gives excellent views. Off Dunny Cove, below Gunrow's Down, we have seen grey seals bottling on a calm summer's day. In addition to the regular birds and flowers, there is a bonus at Stoke, where you can walk above or below Stoke woods. In spring and autumn, migrating warblers, redstarts and flycatchers, goldcrests and firecrests can turn up here, feeding after overnight migration, putting on fat to fuel the next leg of their journey.

The path between Stoke and the mouth of the Erme, at Mothecombe, is not so easy. You can park at the Mothecombe car park and walk both ways along the coast path, or return along the lane, through Alston and Battisborough Cross. The distance is about seven miles. The view across the mouth of the Erme is lovely, no wonder it has been used in several films.

The path between the Erme and the Avon is the most strenuous of any section of the coast path. There are a series of steep climbs and steep descents. I have seen foxes walking in broad daylight through the grass and scrub, on near vertical slopes, nonchalent as ever. Badgers have setts near Beacon Point and the tractor driver, working the fields leading down to the point, has to take care not to overturn his tractor by driving over one of the holes. The Dartmouth slate here is silvery grey and jointed at an acute angle that has produced steep silvery slabs of rock. Peregrines often frequent this part of the coast, confident of seclusion along the hostile cliffs.

There is a path from Kingston down to Wonwell, which then follows the coast path, above the sandy, estuary side to Fernycombe Point and switch-backs along to Wiscombe beach, where there is an interesting beach and caves which are a delight to children. From there you can return to Kingston. From Ringmore, you can walk down to Ayrmer Cove, with its rather gritty, grey sand and along past the caravans and ice creams at Challaborough to Bigbury-on-Sea. Tree mallows, pyramidal orchids and greater knapweed grow along the grassy verges. If you explore Burgh Island, crossing the sands at low tide or catching the Burgh Island tractor at high tide, you can find more pyramidal orchids, near the Pilchard Inn, and, at the far side of the island, cormorants nesting.

The path from Bantham to Thurlestone is popular but always interesting. It is difficult enough to give a sense of achievement but most of the family could attempt it. You can rest half way up the climb from Bantham and admire the view across the mouth of the Avon Estuary. The surfers and wind surfers are there, as well as the sea birds, even in mid-winter. The short grass of the golf course is always a likely place to find a hoopoe, early on a spring morning. Between Warren Point and Leas Foot beach used to be a good place to see

Bantham Beaches and Burgh Island.

occasional little gulls, Sabine's gull and grey phalaropes, in the autumn, after westerly gales. They were attracted by good feeding on the raw sewage outflow. Now the sewage is properly treated and there are less birds! At the top of Leas Foot beach, above the marram grass, are some fine sea holly plants, growing by the old road. You can combine a walk from Thurlestone to Hope Cove and back, with a look at the wetland reserves at South Milton Ley and South Huish marsh. This is easy walking, for the cliffs are low, worn from the softer, Meadfoot beds.

The headland between Leas Foot beach and Thurlestone Sand and the Thurlestone Rock, standing isolated and magnificent out on the wavecut platform, are relics of the New Red Sandstone rocks, which would have once covered all the South Hams. In his novel *The Innocent Moon*, much of which is centred in the South Hams, Henry Williamson calls the Thurlestone Rock 'Britannia Rock' and from certain angles you can imagine Britannia's profile, complete with helmet. He describes the sand dune flowers, where the stream from South Milton Ley, soaks

Thurlestone Rock

through the sands or bursts in flood through them. They are still there today, about seventy years later. On the cliff top grassland, as you pass the first houses of Hope Cove, is some hoary cress. This large, creamy flowered cress is thought to have been brought to the Kentish coast by soldiers returning from the Friesian islands, during the Napoleonic wars, and emptying out their palliasses of Friesian hay. It is not common in the south-west; it does also grow at Sunny Cove at the mouth of Salcombe Harbour. In the bushes and low trees along this coast you are likely to see or hear a cirl bunting. The male's sage-green and brown plumage, with its black bib and eyestripe and its rattling song, that Montagu found monotonous, make it quite easy to separate from a yellowhammer.The females and juveniles are much more difficult, although only yellowhammers have rusty rumps. Andrew Cole, who wrote a splendid book titled *In Search of the Cirl Bunting* in 1993, lived at Hope Cove and did much of his painstaking field-work around Hope Cove and Thurlestone.

From Bolt Tail round to Hallsands, the coast is very different. The rock is schist, not Devon slates. The land is higher; a plateau surface of about 430 feet (130m). The cliffs are mostly sparkling, grainy, mica schist but near Bolt Tail, Salcombe, Rickham, Prawle and Hallsands there are cliffs of the soft green hornblende schist. These are impressive coasts and probably the oldest.

The area from Bolt Tail to Bolt Head was covered by the Soar Bird Report, published annually from 1988 until the early 1990s by Perry Sanders and some two dozen other keen observers. About 150 species of bird were recorded in each year.

Looking, nearly vertically, down at the Bury Stone from Bolt Tail, you can usually see a dozen shags, with a cormorant or two showing up the difference in size between them. About twenty pairs of shags nest along this coast. Around Redrot Cove, named for the red colouration from an outlier of New Red Sandstone, rock sea lavender is frequent and a few patches of golden samphire. Bolt Tail is a good sea watching point. Ducks on the sea may be scoter, which pass by especially in the Spring, but beware, for flocks of wigeon also rest on the sea during the winter. They flight back to the floodwater at South Huish Marsh. On the cliff slopes up to Bolberry Down, broom, as well as gorse, is common. All along the cliffs you may see the creamy-brown spikes of the parasitic broomrape. In our case it is seldom parasitic on broom but on members of the clover family, on ivy or carrot.

Bolberry Down is a particularly attractive heathy area in mid-summer. Grayling butterflies can be prolific by the pathways. Stonechats perch on the top of the gorse bushes, the males smartly plumaged with black head and white collar, the females brown with mellow orange breast. About fifteen pairs usually nest between Bolt Tail and Bolt Head. Yellowhammers are common here, with over a hundred pairs, mostly in the gorse thickets. This is where the grey-backed, wine-purple-fronted Dartford warbler could also nest.

The plateau, inland from the cliff-top, provided an ideal airforce base during both world wars. It is also a traditional site for flocks of golden plover in the winter.

You can head inland, along the lane by the tall masts and return to Hope Cove, making a circular walk of about five miles. From Bolberry you can walk along a ridge for nearly a mile, with the sea on one side and a valley on the other, until you look down to Soar Mill Cove and up the Soar Mill valley. It is a likely area to see wheatears, a few may nest and hundreds pass through on passage.

Down on the beach you can look up into crevices in the cliff-face, where sea spleenwort fern grows. On the grassy slope, leading down to the cliffs above the cove, you may be able to see a dark green ring, about fifty yards across, spreading to the cliff edge. At first I wondered if it were of some prehistoric significance, then, in September, I saw parasol mushrooms growing around its edge. The ring was the fairy-ring, caused by the rotting down of last season's mycelium, as the parasol mushrooms have spread outwards from an original spore, which started over half a century ago. Parasol mushrooms are very common in some years and are delicious fried.

By the path, above the cove, is a gateway with a post rescued from wreckage of a ship. On the gatepost is engraved, "Certified to accommodate 4 seamen". In the days of sail, many ships came to grief along this coast. The late David Murch, in his lectures and in booklets written with his wife Muriel, has chronicled many of these shipwrecks. There is more material on them in the museums in Salcombe and Overbecks at Sharpitor.

You can return to Bolberry Down by turning left up the valley, which is often good for small migrant birds in the thorn and willow scrub. On Hazel Tor, to the right, a peregrine, buzzard or kestrel may be perched. After a stiff climb up from Soar Mill Cove, there is a good level walk with fine views inland to Dartmoor, blue in the distance. Ravens nest on the cliffs.

Whilst walking along The Warren, in September 1991, Alan Doidge saw an unusual bird perched on some bracken. It resembled a large bunting, or lark, but Alan tentatively identified it as a bobolink, a vagrant from America. It was soon confirmed and over a thousand birdwatchers saw it during the four days it remained at The Warren. On several occasions, hoopoes have been seen during spring migration, on the cliff-top and valley grasslands.

Where the path goes down steeply towards the old look out building, chamomile grows in the steep turf, just as it does by some trackways on Dartmoor. At the base of the rocks on your right, in the crevices and overhangs, there is lanceolate, spleenwort growing in a typical location. Round Bolt Head, peregrines are often seen, playing in the wind and flying past on powerful wings. At Bolt Head the small bushes of western gorse, set among heather and flower-starred, rabbit-cropped grassland, look as if they have been planted by a landscape gardener. It is an excellent location for butterflies; Michael Brooking has monitored and mapped the colonies of silver-studded blues, for which this is a traditional site.

Looking eastwards is a wonderful view to Prawle Point, the most southern part of Devon. Bolt Head is a good place from which to look out to sea, for birds and dolphins.

Spring Squill.

Autumn Squill.

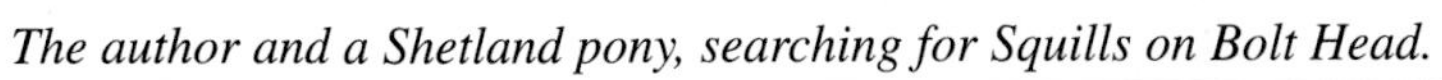

The author and a Shetland pony, searching for Squills on Bolt Head.

The path leads down to the dramatic Starehole Bay. Across the sheltered, blue-green water of the bay rises a jagged line of rocks, called The Rags. Henry Williamson gave them a name more worthy of their dramatic affect – 'Valhalla'. Above the cove itself is a convenient, sheltered beach and on the short grass near the cliff edge is a particularly fine bank of spring squill.

One path leads inland, up the valley, which can be productive for warblers, gold- and firecrests and ring ousels at migration time. The other path, up to 'Valhalla', has lovely plants – bloody cranesbill, ox-eye daisies and wind clipped privet – and the butterflies are excellent. Monica Hazel, when warden of the National Trust at Sharpitor, showed us the privet in scented blossom, surrounded by fluttering dark green fritillaries.

Where the safety railings protect you from the precipice below the ragged rocks, rare lichens, *Roccellas*, sprout from the rock-face. Birdsfoot thrives on the trodden path, as on Dartmoor. From the creeping ivy, by the railing, broomrape and the spiky butcher's broom grow, silhouetted against Starehole's turquoise, wrinkled sea. Out to sea a few gannets may glide and plummet into a shoal of mackerel, Sandwich terns dive and pirouette more energetically, kittiwakes patter the surface in butterfly flight and green-black shags, up to a hundred in the autumn, perch on the rocks or duck-dive in the restless waves.

Shags on the rock.

Both paths continue, one above, one below, along the cliffs to the woods around Overbecks, where you can enjoy a cup of tea and a beautiful garden. From Soar Mill to Overbecks and back is about six miles but you can complete it in parts to make two or three walks of about three miles. From the east side of Salcombe Harbour there are also two paths, an upper and lower, following the coast the two miles to Gara Rock. The cliff-top around Sunny Cove is carpeted with bloody cranesbill. Shags, cormorants and Sandwich terns perch on the rocks and the warning beacons round the Black Stone. Where the lower path emerges from the woods, after Millbay and Sunny Cove, the dappled light, bracken and pignut, bluebells and blue, sun-sparkling sea beyond, are all beautiful in May and June, when butterflies and flowers are at their best. Later there is saw-wort, bell heather, ling and carline thistle. Above Limebury Point, you can look out over the Harbour Bar to Bolt Head – a magnificent view. Sandwich terns may roost here; the most I have ever seen is seventy-five on the rocks together.On the rocks further along the path, below Portlemouth Down, parties of shags, dry out. Even when they are not there, you can tell their favourite rocks, from the whitewash they have left behind.

Martin Catt, a keen naturalist, monitors the wildlife along the cliffs from Gara Rock Hotel to Prawle. He has found the long-fruited birdsfoot trefoil, by the path that descends to the sandy beach at Gara. Cirl buntings nest near the hotel and Dartford warblers skulk in the gorse.

From Gara you can follow an inland path back to Millbay or continue for another mile or so to Pig's Nose, Gammon Head and Macely Cove. The coastal scenery becomes more dramatic as you approach Gammon Head.

At Pig's Nose you enter the area covered by Pete Mayer's excellent book *The Birds of Prawle*. Over the years Devon birdwatchers, like Alan Searle, Dave Norman, Frank Scanlon and Norman Trigg have spent hours walking the footpaths and watching the sea. The results are summarised in Pete Mayer's book and illustrated by Pete Dennis.

If you could walk only one part of the coast, this would be the part to visit. You can spend hours around Elender and Maceley Cove, looking across the idyllic bay to the rugged spur of Gammon Head. The nests of herring gulls and shags are in full sight, on the green, hornblende cliffs. A raven often nests here, bringing wool to line his nest of gorse twigs, on warm February days. You may see a peregrine, sitting majestically on the skyline of Gammon Head. Fulmars and gannets glide by, out to sea.

The flowers are magnificent. Bloody cranesbill is prolific around Maceley Cove; all the common cliff-top flowers are there and linnets twitter in the thick gorse scrub.

The path continues, with glorious views around to the coast-watch look out station on Prawle Point itself. From here you can watch for migration overhead and out to sea. It may take hours before you see anything other than gulls, shags, a few fulmars and gannets but patience is rewarded, particularly after strong winds in the autumn. Auks, razorbills and the browner guillemots fly swiftly and directly by. Occasional skuas, most likely Arctic skuas but sometimes great or pomarine, may harry a flock of kittiwakes to make them disgorge their last meal. A few Balearic, sooty and Cory's shearwaters are seen in most years, gliding, like the fulmar, on stiff wings. I love best the less rare Manx shearwaters, showing first white, then black, as they glide first one way and then the other, almost touching the waves with their wing tips as they change tack. They are one of the few specialities that are most frequent in May and June, when their mates are sitting on eggs or feeding fluffy young down a rabbit burrow on the Isles of Scilly, or other off-shore islands.

The bat-like mother Cary's chickens, the storm petrels, may also appear at this time, fluttering low over the waves. Storm petrels, true to their name, also appear during the equinoctial gales. This is when it is most likely to see rare gulls, such as Sabine's, little and Mediterranean.

Autumn squill is abundant in the short grass around the lookout. This is where Dennis Elphick has seen the autumn ladies tresses orchids, growing amongst the squills. Both are only a few inches high; the one with mauve, pyramidal flower spikes, the other with spiralling cream spires. On the rocks below the point there is a little of the yellow hair lichen – part of a mosaic of grey, brown and orange lichens. Lanceolate spleenwort grows in the shady clefts. In sheltered, sun-trap hollows the bluebells flower early and the whole craggy promontory becomes a colourful rock garden.

Birds of prey are often seen on passage. In addition to the resident kestrels, sparrow hawks, buzzards and peregrine, more join them, passing through, particularly in the autumn. The small, dashing merlin falcons appear then and hobbies also occur every year. In most years a hen harrier is seen, quartering the fields. Rarities have included honey buzzard, black and red kite, marsh and Montagu's harrier, goshawk, osprey and red-footed falcon. It is always worth checking a kestrel perched on telegraph wires, to see if it has red legs.

The best places to search for wading birds are on the wave-cut rocky platforms, revealed off Langerstone Point and Horseley Cove, at low tide. In winter a party of purple sandpiper traditionally returns to the Langerstone Point area, picking over the rocks, together with turnstone. The yellow legs of the sandpipers and the orange legs of the turnstones may be the only part of these well-camouflaged birds you can see. Oystercatchers are often here, with a few curlew, grey plover and occasional redshank, all looking especially attractive and out of place on the sea-weed covered rock. In spring whimbrel stop, on passage, their rapid, quivering cry quite different from curlew. Up on the old First World War airfield, behind the water tower small flocks of golden plover may gather in hard weather and it was here that a pair of dotterel appeared, in May 1982.

In spring you may see swallows arriving over the sea, although the most impressive visible migration is again in the autumn, when thousands of swallows and martins may gather and stream out over the sea, southwards to France, the Sahara, and finally home to South Africa. Early on cloudless autumn mornings is the best time to witness larks, meadow and tree pipits, chaffinches, goldfinches and greenfinches, linnets, siskins and redpolls all flying overhead, journeying to Europe for the winter.

The bushes around the National Trust car park, the Devon Bird Watching and Preservation Society's tiny, private reserve, nearby, and all the hedgebanks and valley scrub are likely places to see small migratory birds skulking. Most of the warblers and flycatchers migrate at night, by the stars, and at dawn they descend into the bushes where they first sight land. Prawle, as the southernmost

View from Prawle Point.

tip of Devon, is a wonderful place to find them, particularly after a clear night which has become cloudy before dawn. Willow warblers, chiffchaffs, blackcaps and whitethroats, spotted and pied flycatchers, redstarts all can suddenly appear in the bushes, sometimes in dozens or even hundreds. Later, in October, numbers of goldcrests appear and a few firecrests, with brilliant white and black eyestripes below their golden crown. Lesser whitethroats, reed and sedge warblers, grasshopper warblers, garden and wood warblers – all are seen in small numbers. The rarities come with them. Almost every year at least one melodious and one icterine warbler are seen at Prawle. Two birds which no longer nest regularly in Britain, the wryneck and the red-backed shrike, pass through. Hoopoes, with their loping flight, raised crest and striking pink and pied plumage, are sometimes seen in spring. There have been several ortolan buntings, red-breasted flycatchers, yellow-browed and Pallas's warblers. The greatest rarities have been the American vagrants, blown across the Atlantic, such as the black and white warbler and the red-eyed vireo.

Singing his rattling, repetitive song from the top of one of these hedges or patches of scrub, where the migrant warblers skulk, may be a sage-green and rich brown bunting, with a black bib and black eye-stripe. This is the cirl bunting, that many bird watchers come especially to see at Prawle. They are present here in a greater density than anywhere else, feeding their young on the abundant grasshoppers and other summer insects. They themselves glean grass and weed seeds from around the edges of the arable fields. One day I should like to possess a jacket woven in the subtle green and browns of a cirl bunting's plumage. The arable fields are on an apron of light, stony soil. This is the head deposit; the result of spring mud-flows, at the end of the last ice age, tumbling over the old cliff line and spreading out below, once extending twenty miles. The soil warms early, on these south-facing coasts and market garden crops, like cauliflowers are grown. These are some of the most productive fields for arable weeds. Musk storksbill, henbit dead-nettle, small nettle and many-seeded goosefoot are all common. Around the edges of the field, hairy birdsfoot trefoil, bloody cranesbill and narrow-leaved everlasting pea clamber up into the grassy banks. Migrant butterflies – clouded yellows and painted ladies – may be especially common here. Along the public footpaths that thread between the fields, the hedges and walls are festooned with honeysuckle and ivy. In autumn, hundreds of red admiral butterflies join the bees, wasps and hover flies around the ivy blossom.

The coast path continues round to Horseley Cove and, after Maelcombe House, rises over an uneven, rocky section to Woodcombe Sand. There is then a good, wide path, past the old coastguard houses to Lannacombe Beach. Tree mallows grow near the head of the beach and a cirl bunting may be singing in the bushes behind the small car park. You can return to Prawle by the path up the Woodcombe valley, to make a circular walk of up to seven miles.

A grassy platform of head stretches between Lannacombe and Great Mattiscombe Sand, giving easy walking and the oportunity to admire the views back to Prawle Point with its rock arch, and the rocky islets off Peartree Point. Just before Mattiscombe, a stream crosses the path. Insects are attracted to the water and the flowering plants, such as fleabane, hemp agrimony, purple loosestrife and great willow-herb. Another stream drops down onto the beach itself. The path curves around its sheltered amphitheatre and you can sit by the path and watch the butterflies floating down onto the flowers and supping their nectar. The head rests on a raised beach, an old wave-cut rocky platform, now about fifteen feet above mean high tide level, and here at Mattiscombe the head has been eroded to form a series of pinnacles.

The path from Mattiscombe to Start Point ranks as one of the most scenically stunning of all our beautiful coast. It is worth waiting on the grassy promontory at Peartree Point, for Atlantic grey seals use the rocks off here to haul out as the tide ebbs. They sleep and scratch and yawn. Their dark pelts turn pale grey as they dry out. The bulls are bigger than the cows and have Roman noses. As the returning tide covers the rocks they are washed off and begin to fish again, surfacing from each long dive, with a snort. They often rest at the surface, floating

Grey Seals

vertically – 'bottling' – this is when they look just like the marker buoys for crab pots!

One spring I was walking around the bay between Peartree and Start Points, when, among the bluebells on the rock-strewn slope, I saw a group of whimbrel. Through the binoculars I could see their dark eye-brows and sharply down-curved beaks pecking among the flowers for insects. There were six of them surrounded by the bowed heads of thousands of bluebells. One looked up and took flight, the rest following, on their way to Shetland or Iceland.

During the winter the cliffs around this bay may be thick with gulls. There may be as many as two thousand great black-backed gulls here, resting shoulder to shoulder by the rocky shore. Suddenly they will take to the air, rising on the buffetting wind and making their wild, barking cries. Sometimes a peregrine, lifting off from the pinnacles above Start Point, will make a long, sloping dive above them.

Herring gulls, fulmars and shags nest on the steep cliffs and shadowed gullies between here and Start Point. Ravens Cove often has a raven's nest. How long ago was it that someone saw ravens nesting here and named the cove? A hundred years, or more? Late stone age flints have been found on Peartree Point, so the ravens' ancestors could have shared this coast with man for very much longer.

The ragged spur of rock, leading down to the sea at Start Point, reminds me of the jagged back of a Stegosaurus. In May, on its southern side, it is painted with pink thrift, red sheep's sorrel, white stars of stonecrop and dark green bushes of gorse dappled with bright yellow blossom. Below the sloping, natural flower garden, the sea – blue or grey – is often white capped, open to the south-westerly wind. On its northern side is a sheet of bluebells, sloping into a quiet bay, protected from the winds of the south and west. As summer progresses bracken grows up tall and thick above it and the stonechats perch on its arching fronds.

Start Point is another good place from which to watch the sea and to record land birds migrating overhead. Swallows, larks, pipits and finches follow the line of the coast southwards from Slapton and Hallsands and fly on, over Start to cross the English Channel. When mist or drizzle comes in before dawn, migrants may be gathered in the bracken and tamarisk bushes near the lighthouse. When there are no stars visible for navigation, they are attracted by the lighthouse beams, sometimes fatally, killing themselves against the glass. Willow warblers, chiffchaffs and perhaps a redstart, with bright red tail will be flitting through the tamarisk. The Saxons who gave the redstart its name, also named this point; it is their word for 'tail'.

Migrants also move up the valley from Mattiscombe to Start Farm; I have seen a wryneck eyeing me quizzically from one of the fence posts. Regular watchers of this patch, like Dave Hopkins, have seen many rare species here – Pallas' warblers and recently Iberian chiffchaff.

There is a narrow road to walk back up from the lighthouse to the car park. Sea storksbill grows on the wall and in the cracks at the side of the road. Ahead, is an impressive view of the coastline, straightened by the shingle bar that stretches nearly six miles, to Strete Gate.

The walk from Start Point car park to Lannacombe and return is about five miles.

As you walk northwards, from the car park towards Hallsands, you can see the pathetic remnants of Old Hallsands village, partially destroyed and unoccupied since 1917. Very little remains of a village that once had a pub and a chapel and was home to over a hundred people. Rock-falls and continuing erosion make it unsafe to descend to the rocky platform on which it was built. In early spring, as you follow the path towards Hallsands, the slope is coloured by spreading patches of creamy yellow primroses, rising from the netted leaves. The golden petalled stars of celandines grow around them. Just before the village is a wild cherry orchard, old trees close-packed in the middle, new suckers spreading on the edges. The blossoms open on bare twigs, against the background of the sky-reflecting sea and make a picture of almost Japanese beauty.

Hallsands.

I still do not know the story of the origin of this orchard but details of the story of Old Hallsands, and of the heroism of Ella Trout can be found at Trouts Hotel – where cream teas and ice cream are on offer too.

A hundred yards beyond Trouts Hotel, stop on the path and listen. Between April and July, you will hear raucous cries of 'Kitti-wake, kittiwake, kitti-waake'! On the crumbling cliffs a colony of several hundred kittiwakes nest here each year. They used to nest at Start Point but they have nearly all moved here and the colony has increased. From the cliff path, near the remnants of the old chapel, you can see some of the nests. Resist the temptation to venture to the cliff edge, or you, like the chapel, will tumble into the sea. Around you is the feathery foliage of tamarisk bushes and tall spires of tree-mallow, head high, with purple flowers like hollyhocks. Below, on the vertical cliff-face, are the muddy nest cups, moulded by the white breasts of the kittiwakes and streaked with their droppings. Their beaks are lemon yellow, their legs, as they stand up, are black. As the males arrived back at the nest there are elaborate greeting ceremonies, with head-nodding and neck-rubbing. The female opens her beak, revealing the bright orange gape and the male regurgitates some love-morsel into her mouth. For a month both birds share the incubation of the two eggs. In June the eggs hatch and in six weeks a transformation takes place from small, fluffy, grey balls to beautifully-marked silver adolescents. No juvenile gull is so handsome as a kittiwake – silver with black accessories; the wings have a zig-zag black line, the tail has a black tip and the neck has a smart, black collar. Young and old spend the winter at sea and it will be about four years before the young first lay their own eggs.

During the winter you may see parties of black, sea ducks – scoter – diving off-shore in Start Bay. Eiders also turn up here and divers, particularly the huge, great northern diver.

Walking down the steep path to Hallsands beach, coltsfoot grows. The bright yellow flowers open in February and the polygon-shaped leaves follow later. It flourishes in light, disturbed soils, so these unstable cliffs are ideal.

The shingle bar, which the sea has pushed up along this east-facing coast, has its own, unique flora. Along it pied wagtails gather, feeding on insects among the plants and rotting seaweed. At dusk there may be a hundred or more at Beesands, Torcross or Slapton Sands. Wheatears are common on migration along the shingle ridge and, at Beesands, there was a desert wheatear, which stayed for several days. Between Beesands and Start Point you can make an interesting cliff walk of about two miles each way.

Where there is erosion of the edge of the shingle bank, the striking yellow-horned poppy comes up, sometimes forming a continuous line of bushes at the foot of the miniature erosion-cliff. They are showy plants, with glaucous leaves, floppy, yellow flowers and curved seed pods, like cows' horns. They also flourish in scree, where the cliffs have fallen and on the coastal spoil heaps beside the entrance to Beesands Quarry, where they grow with mulleins.

Where the shingle is building up sea spurge and sand couch grass are often the pioneer species, followed by rest-harrow. All of these plants respond to accretions of shingle by rapidly putting down roots. The rest-harrow is particularly effective at the northern end of Slapton Sands. You can see circular patches of the plant spreading over the bare shingle with the small, pink pea flowers more vigorous around the circumference. In the middle of the rest-harrow patches, as the centre dies, new plants in the succession become established, like the little maritime grass, darnel fescue. Gradually these patches of rest-harrow are coalescing, until a continuous sward will be established.

There are occasional pioneering plants of sea-kale and sea holly. Sea-pea once grew here. There are several other members of the pea and clover family,

Above: Restharrow colonising the bare shingle – with close-up.

Below: Vipers Bugloss, with Sea Radish in the foreground.

including rest-harrow, that grow in the shingle-ridge sward. All of them manufacture their own nitrogenous fertiliser, using atmospheric nitrogen and the nitrogen-fixing nodules on their roots; an ideal adaptation for growing in areas poor in humous and nutrients.

Burnet Moths on Ragwort.

Birdsfoot trefoil is very common, so there are common blue butterflies and the red and black six-spot burnet moths, whose larvae feed on the birdsfoot trefoil and the adults flock to the flowery ragwort. Towards the Torcross end of Slapton Sands thrift is abundant, and by the roadside there the blue flowers of chickory have become naturalised.

The broken seashells and snailshells among the shingle produce enough calcium to enable several chalk-loving plants to thrive. Ladies bedstraw, creeps through the other herbage and produces small, yellow clouds of blossom and, where it is growing near hedge bedstraw, the hybrid between the two occurs. The most striking plant that grows on both sides of the road, betweeen Torcross and Strete Gate, is vipers bugloss. It grows in dense patches and its spikes are brilliant blue and purple.

As the sward becomes established and more rank, red fescue grass becomes dominant with almost 'wall-to-wall' sea-radish. This tall, bushy plant has pale yellow flowers and seed pods that the greenfinches love to plunder. Although it is so common here, nationally it is a rarity.

At the far end of the straight road, there is car parking at Strete Gate. On the shingle, near the car park, are several naturalised plants of sea daffodil, a native of Mediterranean shores. Perhaps one day it will become as common as the red valerian, which looks so much at home on the rocky slopes behind.

The paths through the clearings and buddleia-rich scrub, around the car park, are good for butterflies and it was here that several monarch butterflies were seen a few years ago.

Passing down the coast, out to sea, especially in spring and autumn, are hundreds of gulls, including kittiwakes, terns, gannets, occasional skuas and flocks of scoter. The scoter may be seen in the winter too, with great northern diver and sometimes Slavonian grebe.

To walk the whole length of Slapton Sands from Torcross to beyond Strete Gate and back, is about six miles.

Apart from the popular beach at Blackpool Sands, there is no public access to the coast between Strete and Stoke Fleming but there is a National Trust car park near Little Dartmouth, just east of Stoke Fleming, and from there a beautiful path takes you round to Dartmouth Castle at the mouth of the River Dart.

From the car park the path runs down to above Warren Point and meanders around points and coves, with beautiful views of the rocky coast. The rich aerial insect life above the meadows and scrubland in the valley leading down to Compass Cove attracts martins and swallows in the autumn.

As you wind down and around to the Castle, for the first time, wild cabbage becomes a common plant of the cliff flora. But my favourite part of this walk is where, after Compass Cove, the path descends to the rocky platform of a raised beach. A wooden bridge takes you across a deep gulley onto the flat rocks. In sea caves, beneath your feet, the breaking waves echo and rumble, like the snoring of a sleeping giant. Over the rocks, thrift, sea spurrey and plantain make a rock garden. There are views out to Western Blackstone, where shags will be perched. You can look down into the sea, where the seaweeds sway and small fish dart. There is time to sit and contemplate, among the sea pinks, listening to the sound of the sea.

IX

THE SEASHORE AND THE SEA

Butterfish

Standing on the shore at Horseley Cove, Thurlestone, Mattiscombe or Bantham, the waves curl and break over the wavecut platform of rock. These rocks were sediments beneath the sea about 400 million years ago. Devon's geology continues here as new layers of sand accumulate beneath the sea, perhaps to be raised as rock in millions of years' time.

Left along the tide-line are seaweeds, litter and hints of earlier and other creation. There are mermaid's purses, black or brown pouches with tendrils at each corner, which contained the young of rays or dogfish. White, oval 'bones' are the internal skeletons of cuttlefish – strange fish-like molluscs that prey on crustaceans and hide from predators in a puff of sepia smoke of their own making. What appear to be bath sponges made of papery bubbles are groups of whelk egg-cases; the young have hatched, eaten most of their siblings and drifted away into the plankton. Dead and dying jellyfish and their allies lie among the flotsam and jetsam. The transparent, common jellyfish have four violet rings at their centre. The larger compass jellyfish have brown lines dividing the round body into segments, like a compass rose, and brown dots around the circumference. They have many fine tentacles and four long trailing ones that sting and earn it the name of sea nettle. Transparent, rigid ovals, with a half moon sail, are by-the-wind-sailors, Sometimes some of their blue tentacles survive; they and all jelly-fish like animals use their tentacles to ensnare and paralyse the plankton, on which they feed. By-the-wind-sailors are blown across the Atlantic, sometimes being washed up in hundreds. After the autumn gales, pieces of wood or plastic, from which hang dozens of goose barnacles – shiny, black necks, capped by white shells – are also brought to our shores from mid-Atlantic. From mediaeval times, it was thought that the black-necked, white-throated geese that came each autumn to western Scotland and Ireland, hatched from these peculiar barnacles. To this day the geese are called barnacle geese. On the sandy shore, sea potatoes are often washed up – brittle, white baubles, the shells of the sea-urchin, which lives beneath the sand.

Goose Barnacles.

A flock of turnstones, orange legs scampering over the stranded seaweed, walk along the tide-line, flicking over the weed and snapping up the sand-hoppers underneath. One of the sandhoppers, *Talitrus saltator*, was first described by George Montagu. Pecking in the tideline litter there are dark brown, sparrow-sized birds. They have grey outer tail feathers and feed on the invertebrates that live among the rotting seaweed. Montagu was the first to describe these birds – they are rock pipits. As the tide begins to ebb, you can explore the world between the tides, firstly looking at the bare rock. On exposed shores, in crevices around high tide mark, small winkles are clustered, like grape-purple pips. Clustering in cracks at and below this level are the slightly bigger, rough winkles, deeply grooved in this exposed situation and varying in colour from grey to orange-yellow. Lower down, browsing on the bare rock, on the middle shore and at the edge of rock pools, are the larger edible winkles and thick topshells. Thick topshells are sometimes called toothed winkles, on account of the mother-of-pearl ringed opening, with a tooth-like projection at the side. The bluntly pointed top, where it is worn, also has mother-of- pearl showing through the dark colouring.

Barnacles give a grey-white speckling to the bare rock of the upper and middle shore. They are crustaceans, which begin their lives floating in the plankton, looking very like the planktonic stage of shore crabs. Later, they glue themselves, head downwards, to the bare rock and live out their lives sweeping for microscopic plankton, with their feathery 'legs'. Barnacles higher on the shore are mostly *Chthamalus*. There are two similar species; one named in honour of George Montagu has a kite-shaped opening. From the middle shore, most of the barnacles are *Semibalanus balanoides*, and they have a diamond-shaped opening. Lowest of all, especially on rocky overhangs, are the sparsely spread, volcano-shaped species called *Balanus perforatus*. There is a smaller, greyer barnacle, with only four plates, instead of the usual six, making up the 'volcano'. This *Elminius modestus* is a barnacle from New Zealand, which first appeared on British shores in about 1940. It now occurs all round Britain, especially in estuaries.

Larger than barnacles and stuck to the rock, like Chinamen's hats, are limpets; shellfish that rasp the algal slime from the rocks at high tide and return to their home patch, as the tide falls. So faithfully do they return that they wear a ring, where their shell clamps down on the rock. The off-white molluscs with pointed shells, that are often found near barnacles and limpets, are dog-whelks. They rasp away at the protective shells of the barnacles and limpets and suck out the soft body inside.

Following the tide's retreat, where the exposure to the waves is less, there are zones of seaweed, as on the rocky, estuarine shores: a narrow zone of channel wrack, a rather wider zone of spiral wrack, a very wide zone of knotted wrack, a little bladder wrack and finally the serrated wrack, with its edge as serrated as a saw blade.

Flat winkles, beautifully camouflaged as yellow, green or brown bladders, browse on these wracks. Especially on the saw wrack, tiny, white whirls are stuck to the fronds. These are the chemically made tubes of the spiral tube-worms. Longer, snaky ones on and under the rocks are the tubes of serpent tube-worms.

Where the knotted or saw wracks overhang deep gullies, in thick curtains, a swish of the curtain will reveal a wonderworld. Bright orange and pale green sponges spread over the wet rock and weep water at a touch. Montagu named one of the orange varieties and studied them in his microscope. Deep red beadlet anemones and the green spotted, strawberry variety, hang as drooping, rubbery bulbs, their tentacles withdrawn inside. Various small, red seaweeds – flat tongues, ferny branches, fronds made of little,red sausages, even some pale pink ones with white bags attached, which are purse sponges – all hang down the rock as part of a purple-red tapestry. Let go the curtain of saw wrack and the magical world is completely hidden again.

In depressions and gullies in the rocky platforms, rock pools are scattered as colourful oases. Each rock pool is unique – a miniature world of beauty. Most are lined with a pink-purple skin of *Lithophyllum* – purple rockweed. Tufts of *Corallina* weed, resemble stiff, pink-branched bushes. Sea lettuce floats up from the purple floor. as translucent, green tongues. The dense, dark-purple, branching fronds of carragheen moss are stunted, but rising high above them, through the still water are tall, green velvet antlers of Codium weed. In the deeper pools, rainbow weed may grow, shining irridescently blue, green, yellow and orange. If you lift it from the water, the colour vanishes and it is a limp beige weed.

Gliding over the skin of purple rockweed, are purple top shells, their flattened shells decorated with delicate lines of purple and green over a pearly background. Beadlet anemones open their flowers of red tentacles, waiting for the prawns to venture too close and be ensnared. The buff or green tentacles, tipped with purple, are those of snakelocks anemones. They cannot withdraw their tentacles, so they spread perpetually and, like Medusa's hair, are fatally attractive. Hiding under overhanging ledges, or in the thickest weeds are shore crabs, brown or green, scuttling sideways into a new shelter, when disturbed.

On the weeds sea-slugs may climb. Montagu discovered several new species, including the green one, *Elysia viridis,* which is often found on sea lettuce. Grey sea-slugs, sea hares, which produce a purple dye, and the yellow sea-lemons are some of the more common sea-slugs. Some sea-slugs feed on anemones.

Hidden in corners and crannies of the rock pools may be small fish, such as the shanny, or common blenny, the blue spotted Montagu's blenny and the fatherlasher, or scorpion fish, with bony crest and spines.

Living on the surface film are very small, blue springtails, usually gathered in clusters; one of the very few insects to be adapted to life between the tides. These inhabitants of the rock pools are as strange as aliens from another planet.

As the tide sinks to its lowest ebb, a new and even stranger habitat emerges from the sea. From rubbery buttons, yellow cords of thong weed, ten feet long or more, rise up from the rock and float, coiled on the surface. These are washed up like heaps of spaghetti along the tide-line in the autumn gales. They are biennials. In the first year all that grows is the rubbery button. The second year is a celebration of sex – ten feet of fertile spore producing frond. Below these and the saw wrack zone, is a forest of arching stems, from which spread fingers of oar weed, like giants' hands, swaying in the surge of the waves. Most are the common oarweed but there will be some furbellows – another annual – which has a knobbly, hollow holdfast, and some sea belt, a single, ribbed frond that children sometimes call 'crocodile tail weed'. Living within the holdfasts and browsing on the oarweed fronds are especially beautiful shellfish, blue rayed limpets. When young they are almost transparent with three irridescent blue rays.

At this low level, the low water of spring tides, carefully lift the boulders lying in the gulleys and the carpet of seaweed. Having glimpsed their secrets, replace them, very gently and with respect, for the creatures who hide beneath them are nearly all very fragile. When you first look at the under surface of a boulder, it may appear barren. Look more carefully and you will see many animals, pressed close to the rock and well camouflaged. There are brittle stars, with a disc, from which extend five, sinuous arms. Cushion stars are usually pale green and shaped like five cornered cushions, with the corners hardly extended at all. A small, brown relative of the lobster – the broad-clawed porcelain crab – is common under boulders. Its hairy body and claws are flattened, the long feelers are swept back and any part of it can break off, like fine porcelain.

In the cavity, where you have lifted a boulder, may be a pink, pointed shell, the painted topshell, the largest of its family. It may contain its proper owner, or it may be an empty shell that has been taken over by a hermit crab. If you wait

Fiddler Crab on Purple Rock Weed and a Carrageen Moss.

long enough, he will come out of his shell, first his eyes, on stalks, then his lobster claws and finally his legs to carry himself and his home scuttling for safety. You may also surprise crabs; sometimes brick-red, pie-crust shelled, edible crabs or, more often, fiddler crabs. Fiddler crabs hold their claws open, in fear and aggression, as if about to take up a violin and bow. They have startlingly red eyes and broad, fringed back legs, with beautiful violet-blue markings, adapted for swimming. Their shell, if you dare touch it, is soft to the touch, like velvet, and so they can be called velvet swimming crabs.

On the under sides of boulders and on the overhanging walls of the deep gulleys, near low water, are star ascidians – mats of colourless or milky jelly, with stars of blue or orange shining through. These are colonial sea-squirts; the planktonic larvae have a primitive backbone, just as we had, when first fertilised in the waters of our mother's womb.

Near the sea, where it is wet beneath the boulders, there may be fish. Two eel-like fish, both often reddish in colour, are the five bearded rockling, that has barbels, like a catfish, and the butterfish, which has a line of dark, oval blotches down the dorsal fin. The Cornish sucker fish is easily recognised by the two turquoise, false eye spots on top of the flattened head. Montagu's sea-snail is plainer but similar, holding itself down on the rock with a sucker-like pad.

Out in the water, through a mask, I have looked down on shoals of sand-eels; silver arrows, shooting through the oarweed forest. Ballan wrasse, green and red, in almost tropical splendour swim along the edge of the oarweeds. These nest-building fish may begin life as females and later develop into males, to end their days.

Every summer basking sharks swim close inshore, their triangular, dorsal fins cleaving the surface. They swim slowly, their huge mouths wide open to catch the drifting plankton; they are completely harmless. Little is known of their breeding habits or their distribution in the winter. Bigbury Bay is a regular stronghold for summer shoals of basking sharks in Devon. Mick Loates has seen them most frequently from Bolt Tail. The adults can be over twenty feet (six metres) long. A young one, a mere nine feet long, came right below him. The whole fish was visible through the clear water and its slowly beating tail nearly touched the surf-laced rocks.

The tide turns and floods again. Pulsing by and heading back out to sea is a huge jellyfish. It has a white, rounded bell, bigger than a football and eight, fluffily thickened arms stream out behind it, tinged blue. The jellyfish is our largest, *Rhisostoma octopus*. Two hundred years ago George Montagu found one of these jellyfish and examined it in close detail. Living inside he found a green-eyed shrimp, *Hyperia*, which no-one had ever found before.

Montagu has influenced so many naturalists in Devon. A hundred years ago E.A.S.Elliot was writing, *Notes on Birds in the South Hams District* in the transactions of the Devon Association, acknowledging his debt to Montagu.

There are two naturalists, John Cranch and Hugh Cuming, who worked with Montagu, at the beginning of the Nineteenth Century. They were particularly attracted to the seashore and sea life. For them George Montagu was a father figure. As boys they helped him dig for worms and shellfish along the seashore and trawl for fish out from Salcombe. After Montagu's death, in 1815, John Cranch joined a naval expedition to the Congo, as ship's zoologist and sadly died there, of fever. Hugh Cuming emigrated to South America. He gained a mistress in Valparaiso and made his fortune, so that he was able to build himself a seagoing ship. He set out on voyages catching and collecting fish, seashells and other creatures, around South America and to Polynesia and the Philippines. When he died, in 1846, his collection of shells was purchased by the British Museum for £6,000 – a vast sum. As we explore the rock pools we are following in their footsteps, although we will probably not die of fever in a distant land, make our fortunes or find a mistress in Valparaiso.

The South Hams has been a place of discovery since Montagu's day and will continue to be so, for the search for knowledge and the pleasure it brings, continues endlessly and, as George Montagu wrote, "The days of darkness are now passed, when the researches of the naturalist were considered as trivial and uninteresting." *Testacea Britannica* 1803.

Good hunting!

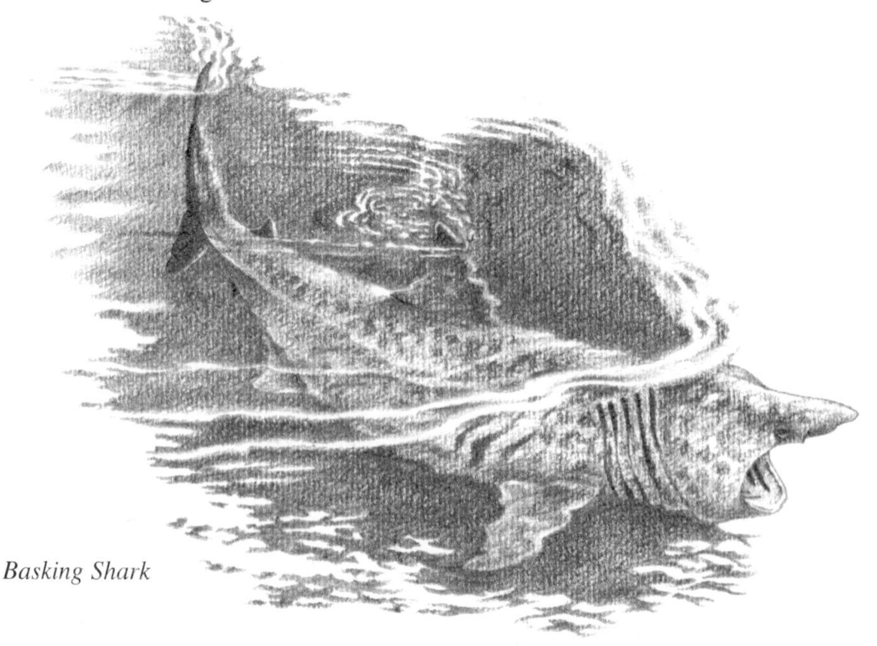

Basking Shark

BIBLIOGRAPHY

Coast & Countryside Service of South Hams District Council

Self guided walks leaflets on:

Aveton Gifford, Dartmouth, Ermington, Kingsbridge, Kingsbridge & Salcombe Estuary, Modbury, Rattery, Salcombe and Totnes.

Dart Valley Trail and Erme Valley Trail

South West Coast Path – Guides for Walkers

Cycling and Mountain Biking in the South Hams

Devon Bird-Watching and Preservation Society. *Devon Bird Report.*

Annual reports available from 1983 and Atlas of Breeding Birds.

Kingsbridge and District Natural History Society. *Annual Report.*

Transactions of the Devon Association

Elliot,E.A.S. (Many articles between 1897 and 1925)

A Century's Work on Ornithology in the Kingsbridge District Vol.29 1897

Twelve Months Notes on Birds in the South Hams District Vol.31, 32, 34, 36, 44, 45, 48, 50. (1899–1918)

The Pilchard Fishery at Borrough Island – Col.Montagu's notes Vol.35 1903.

Twenty Years' Record of the Arrival of Spring Migratory Birds in the Neighbourhood of Kingsbridge Vol.36 1904

Some Birds of Interest on Dartmoor Vol. 46 1914

The Natural History of the Sors (Bolt Tail to Bolt Head) Vol 47

Notes on the Natural History of Start Bay Vol. 56 1925

White,W.W, Hurrell,H.G. & Wynne-Edwards,V.C.
Second Report of Devon Bird-Watching and Preservation Society Vol.62 1930

Smith, Sir Eric *Some Early Nineteenth Century Devonshire Naturalists* (George Montagu, William Leach, Hugh Cuming & John Cranch) Vol.112 1980

The Journal of the Field Studies Council Vol.8 No. 4 July 1996 (Issue dedicated to Slapton Ley)

Elphick, Dennis *A review of 35 years of bird-ringing at Slapton Ley (1961–1995)*

Kennedy, C.R. *The Fish of Slapton Ley*

Riley, Chris *Mammals and other animals.*

Other Published Works

Boot, Kelvin and Franks, Elaine *West Country Wildlife – A Naturalist's Year in Devon and Cornwall* George Philip, London 1992.

Ann Born *A History of Kingsbridge and Salcombe* Phillimore 1986
Bristow,C, Mitchell S., Bolton D.E. *Devon Butterflies* Devon Books 1993
Cleevely,R.J. *Some background into the life and publications of Colonel George Montagu* Journal of Social Bibliography, 1978.
Cole, Andrew *In Search of the Cirl Bunting* Sutton, Stroud 1993
Durrance E.M. and Laming D.J.C. *The Geology of Devon* University of Exeter 1982
Fitzgerald, J. *Off the Map – around the Kingsbridge, Salcombe and Dart Estuaries* Green Books 2000
Fox, Sarah Prideaux *Kingsbridge Estuary, with Rambles in the Neighbourhood* Kingsbridge 1864 and reprinted by Cookworthy Museum Society
Harvey, L.A. & St.Leger-Gordon, D. *Dartmoor* Collins New Naturalist, London 1962
Hurrell, Elaine *Watch the Otter* Country Life Books 1963.
Hurrell, H.G. *Atlanta My Seal* William Kimber, London 1963.
Wildlife: Tame but Free David & Charles 1968.
Ivimey-Cook, R.B. *Atlas of the Devon Flora* Devon Association 1984
Mayer, P. M. *The Birds of Prawle* Kingsbridge 1993
Montagu, George *Ornithological Dictionary & Supplement* 1802 & 1813.
Testacea Britannica 1803
Moore, Robert *The Birds of Devon* David & Charles 1969
Norman, Dave and Tucker, Vic *Where to Watch Birds in Devon and Cornwall* Helm, London 1991.
Perkins, John W. *Geology Explained in South and East Devon.*
Geology Explained: Dartmoor and the Tamar Valley David and Charles 1971 and 1972
Proctor, M. C. F. *The Phytogeography of Dartmoor Bryophytes* – from *Dartmoor Essays* Devonshire Association 1964.
Sanders,P. (editor) *The Soar Bird Report* Kingsbridge 1988–92
Sitters, H. *Tetrad Atlas of the Breeding Birds of Devon* Devon Bird Watching and Preservation Society, 1988
Soper, Tony *The Wildlife of the Dart Estuary* Harbour Books 1986
Waterhouse, Gordon *Wildlife of the Salcombe & Kingsbridge Estuary* New edition: Orchard Publications, Newton Abbot 1999.
Westcott, Stephen *The Grey Seals of the West Country* Truro 1997

GENERAL INDEX

INDEX OF PLANTS

INDEX OF BIRDS